Light
AT THE
Beginning
OF THE
Tunnel

MOSAICA PRESS

Light

AT THE

Beginning

OF THE

Tunnel

WIRING OUR CHILDREN FOR HAPPINESS

BETH PERKEL

ISBN: 978-1-952370-14-4

Published by Mosaica Press, Inc.
www.mosaicapress.com
info@mosaicapress.com

אוֹר זָרֻעַ לַצַּדִּיק וּלְיִשְׁרֵי לֵב שִׂמְחָה
"Light is sown for the righteous, happiness
for the upright."

In memory of our beloved parents, who took the light of
Torah and mitzvos from their ancestors and faithfully
projected its radiance upon us, providing illumination to
guide us through the innumerable challenges of life

Rabbi Solomon Pollack הרב שלמה יהודה פולק

Mrs. Malvina Pollack מלכה פרומעט פולק

Mr. Harry Glassenberg צבי הירש גלסנברג

Mrs. Muriel Glassenberg שיינה מלכה גלסנברג

Dedicated in loving memory by
Harold and Sharon Pollack

אייר תשע"ב

לכבוד רבני,

The book "Light at the Beginning of the Tunnel — Teaching Children the Foundations of Happiness" by Mrs. Beth Perkel, wife of our esteemed colleague Rabbi David Perkel, is a wonderfully written and Torah-based primer on the important mitzvah of חינוך, of raising our children properly. I once heard from a grandson of Rabbi Avrohom Pam zt"l that when a father brought his young son to Rabbi Pam for a blessing that his son be successful in becoming a brilliant Torah scholar, Rabbi Pam responded that the more appropriate blessing, which he would confer, was that the son should derive great happiness from Torah study. Mrs. Perkel's book adeptly and systematically teaches how to ingrain שמחת חיים, a sense of inner happiness and calm in our children, so that they can attain their full potential in the service of Hashem. With Torah blessings,

Yona Reiss

Table of Contents

ACTION

ENVIRONMENT

Section Three

Light at the Middle of the Tunnel

Section Four

Forming Your Tool Kit

Acknowledgments

Writing this book posed a strange problem that I never expected to encounter with one of the biggest undertakings of my life. To put my ideas on paper and glean the gems of wisdom shining through the dusty gravel of my life thus far, I actually had to step out of my own head with all of its racing thoughts and preconceived notions. *But how exactly do you write a book without being in your own head?* you may ask, quite fairly. *In fact, how exactly do you do **anything** without being in your own head?* The answer I have found is simply realizing that there is no other way. By sitting in front of the daunting computer screen as a thousand different cranial call-outs voice their opinions as to what you should write, you then realize that the only way you can go forth with clarity and candor is to turn off your head entirely and simply write from your heart.

I have learned so much from writing this book. Lesson one is that sometimes we need to turn down our inner volume, the self-consciousness and over-consciousness, to truly hear the wisdom that whispers quietly within us. And so, what you have before you is entirely the whisperings from within, the true nuggets that have guided my parenting, my life, and (this year) my fingers across the keyboard to fill that blank computer screen with the insight of what my heart has to say: my candor, my clarity, my lessons-learned-from-mistakes-turned ink. My understanding of the immense research out there on the topic of happiness and how it applies to us today as Jewish parents, charged with the daunting task of helping our children navigate a complex world.

Lesson two is that while an author's name gets to shine brightly on a cover, a book is by no means created alone. First and foremost, I cannot offer enough thanks to the second half of my *neshamah*—my beloved husband Dovid—who helped me so much with both gathering the sources and acting as a sounding board for this book. As the saying goes, when I count my blessings, I always count you twice. It's nothing short of miraculous how we ended up meeting each other after I got lost on my first day at university and stopped you, a random stranger, for directions. I was merely nineteen years old. Since then, you have provided direction in my life in matters much more critical than finding the way to my apartment; so much of my wisdom and outlook on life comes from having learned it, lived it, or talked it over with you by my side. Your patience is bountiful and you have been a light to me at every stage of the tunnel we have traveled through together thus far.

Next, I would like to thank my beloved children. It is for you that I have gathered these ideas that I now share with the world. It says in *Pirkei Avos* (4:20) that teaching children is like writing on a blank slate, but I think for a parent this description is even more fitting: When you become a parent you suddenly realize how much you don't know about the world. *You* become a blank slate that your children ultimately write on—you learn so much from them because ultimately you are both teaching each other. Thank you, my precious crew, for all you have taught me about life, love, and happiness. And thank you for the opportunity to be your chef, chauffeur, teacher, alarm clock, mediator, entertainer, janitor, personal assistant, wardrobe stylist, concierge, stain removal expert, champion tickler, and even napkin when necessary. My husband likes to quote an incident when someone asked me how it felt to be a mother and I answered, "It feels like everything." There is joy, pride, elation, and awe...but also anxiety, overwhelm, and many other seemingly opposite emotions. And yet, the cholent of emotions is a complex-recipe-turned-sweet when you turn your beautiful eyes up to me or slip your buttery-soft, warm hands in mine and whisper, "Love you, Ima!"

I would be remiss if I did not thank my own parents as well. Thank you for all the love and guidance, and for being the biggest cheerleaders for my writing career since I decided to pursue it in first grade. Thank you for chasing and purchasing magazines with me around the globe when my articles have been published, for the pride you take when I win a writing award, for holding the lighting screens when extra hands are needed for a photo shoot to accompany an article, and of course, for editing that crucial word in my college essay.

Thank you to my editor Rabbi Doron Kornbluth and the rest of the dedicated staff at Mosaica Press for all their tireless work in bringing this book and my vision for it to life. Thank you to the online newspaper *The Times of Israel* for hosting my *Light at the Beginning of the Tunnel* blog, from which several chapters in this book have been adapted.

Acharon acharon chaviv—the last one being the most precious, thank You, Hashem, Master of the Universe. Before I write, I often turn my heart heavenward and pray for *"pischon peh"*—for Hashem to open my mouth with the right words to inspire people through my writing and bring them closer to their Creator. I often invoke the liturgical beauty from the following prayer in the Rosh Hashanah davening, as I find it particularly poignant as I seek Divine assistance with my writing:

לְאָדָם מַעַרְכֵי לֵב וּמֵה׳ מַעֲנֵה לָשׁוֹן. ה׳ שְׂפָתַי תִּפְתָּח וּפִי יַגִּיד תְּהִלָּתֶךָ.

The thoughts in man's heart are his to arrange, but the tongue's eloquence comes from Hashem. O Hashem, open my lips, so that my mouth may declare Your praise.

This says it all. Often, man is left struggling to find the right words, because it is Hashem who controls language. I know I am ultimately Hashem's mouthpiece to get messages across through my writing, and I am so grateful for all the success He has given me thus far through my words.

Beth Perkel

בתיה רחל פרקל

Introduction

There is a famous saying that applies to someone approaching the end of something difficult: he or she sees "the light at the end of the tunnel." The saying comes from the many accounts of people with near-death experiences (many of whom were considered medically dead for several seconds or even minutes before they were revived), who describe seeing a light beckoning to them at the end of a long tunnel before they reentered the land of the living. After these accounts became famous, the term colloquially came to mean seeing the end of a task near completion.

This saying always made me reflect on two things:

- The tunnel brought to my mind the famous *prozdor* from the Mishnah in *Pirkei Avos* (4:16) that describes how this world is like a hallway leading into the banquet room of the World to Come. The Mishnah encourages us to prepare ourselves in this entryway hall (during our lifetime) before we walk into the banquet (after our death). It seems fitting, then, that a tunnel is seen as one leaves this world and heads toward the real party.

- The second thing that always fascinated me was the type of light that beckoned to people as they left this world. Individuals who had near-death experiences often described the light as very calming and clear, pulling the person exactly where they needed to go.[1] But where was this light all along? We could certainly have used some spotlights to illuminate what paths we should have

---

1   John C. Hagan and Raymond A. Moody, *The Science of Near-Death Experiences* (Columbia: University of Missouri Press, 2017).

1

taken in this world to make it to the banquet in the first place! Our great rabbis, *Chazal*, often compared our world to darkness; and so, isn't this dark hallway where the light is needed most, as we straighten our proverbial ties (character traits) and smooth out the wrinkles in our clothes (deeds) over 120 years for the luckiest of us *prozdor*-preparers?

Of course, we need light here in this world, but we need to find it on our own—using our own power generator, if you will. The good news though, is reflected in one of my favorite sayings: "This world is full of light, it is we that cast the shadows." God never leaves us in total darkness in this world. Even in Noach's *teivah* (ark) there was an *even tovah*, a unique stone, which *Rashi* says was a special gem that gave off light for those stuck inside. And even the prophet Yonah had a heaven-sent light to illuminate the world for him when he was in the belly of the whale.

The point is that light is all around us, we just need to learn how to harness it to illuminate our way as we muddle through the hallway that is this world. Joy and, more broadly, the Hebrew term *menuchas hanefesh* (peace of mind) are two facets of that light that God has given us, two gifts that work together and help us succeed as our "happiness system." The thing is that both are skills, both are an *avodah* that has to be worked for. In other words, we need to learn to wire our internal circuits for the lights to turn on. And this wiring begins in childhood. The good news is that in childhood our brain is busy wiring its circuits anyway. In fact, in the first few years of life alone, more than one million new neural connections form every second. Early experiences affect the development of the brain architecture, which provides the foundation for all future learning, behavior, and health. And therefore, childhood is the perfect time to build the happiness system from the ground up, as opposed to having to rewire it later in life. The skills for happiness create tremendous potential for our youth that literally can be life-saving lights at the beginning of the tunnel.

My guess is that you've seen the rows and rows of books—in your local library or through the window as you pass a bookstore—authored by happiness gurus peddling their wares. And yet somehow, here we are, you and me (and hopefully a quiet moment) with this particular book in hand. My unique goal here is to sift through those other books and highlight the most salient research to help us address this timely topic of our generation from a Jewish perspective.

The truth is that we are just in the nick of time. Many of our children are drowning in the crashing waves of our larger society that puts a value on instant gratification and whitewashes our realities by continuously putting forth the best image (be it real or fake). This sparks a primal need for the next thing that will bring us happiness, all the while creating a bigger chasm of mental chaos.

In my time as a student at the University of Pennsylvania, I participated in all kinds of psychology research and study, but the research that fascinated me the most pertained to people's dispositions and happiness. What was so exciting about being at this particular university in the early 2000s was that it was the research home of Martin Seligman, the man credited as being the father of "positive psychology." This was the beginning of the emergence of the field and its efforts to scientifically explore human potential, including positive thoughts, behaviors and emotions (like happiness). Seligman published *Authentic Happiness* in 2002 when I was a freshman, and I was very excited about what this new field might uncover about how we could directly approach the idea of lasting happiness.

Life takes you on many roads through the long-winding *prozdor*, and I gave up my research roles when I happily got married and moved to Israel just a few weeks after graduation so my husband could learn Torah full time. But I never lost my interest in the rapidly developing field of positive psychology, and I closely followed its growth and ideas over the years, marveling at how much of it overlaps with Torah thoughts.

After we moved back to America and I became a rebbetzin in 2008, I began to give *shiurim* in the community. I would weave in positive psychology as viewed through the prism of Torah. At the time I was a young mother, and as my family grew, I began to see via personal experience the importance of working on the building blocks for happiness with my children from the earliest ages. Finally, in 2012, I began to condense my ideas and write what became a popular blog on teaching children happiness. Little did I know at the time that the seeds would blossom into this book. Now more than ever, this generation needs to address our topic head-on. The coronavirus has wreaked havoc on our world, and one of the many facets of its impact is the mental health crisis that has been left in its wake. The struggle to reestablish our equilibrium makes reviewing the material presented here all the more critical. Even if you have previously learned about some of the ideas that are presented here, it is very powerful to relearn and review them as we strive to strengthen our families' contentment and happiness muscles after going through this challenging period of time.

What is unique about my perspective is that I will show you how many of the popular positive psychology components of happiness-building fit in with Torah ideas, and we will be viewing them through the prism of the great rabbinic teachings of *Chazal*. There will be exercises to help us obtain a richer level of understanding of our children as individuals, and subsequently help them in a targeted way. My goal is to help you think deeper about what might be getting in the way of your children's happiness and to help remedy this with specific strategies. As I will discuss in section 1, children growing up in this generation (and likely subsequent generations as well) have unique challenges when it comes to happiness that were not experienced in previous generations.

The detailed approach I take in this book is one of creating a "light at the beginning of the tunnel" for our children, to help them grow with happiness skills and well-adjusted foundations. This requires a four-pronged method. Each will have its own dedicated section:

1. Understanding the deeper definitions of terms that are often thrown around but seldom defined, such as "growth," "personality types," and even the term "happiness" itself.

2. Educating ourselves about, and working toward, planting specific happiness seeds in our children (grit, acceptance, gratitude, emotional agility, mindfulness, patience, and several more) as well as working on specific outer matters as parents that will support the sprouting of these happiness seeds (setting up the physical home for happiness, slowing down the rush of our daily

lives, letting ourselves become comfortable with letting our children fail, to name a few), along with actions for growing and maintaining this abundant happiness crop (tackling vulnerability, reducing complaining, identifying strengths, getting quality sleep, and more). The ideas in this section will be divided into three subsections that create an all-encompassing approach for happiness: mind, action, and environment.

3. Learning key components of pursuing and successfully achieving our own happiness that will trickle down to our children.

4. Finding targeted tools to support ourselves in this journey, as parents, toward greater family happiness.

It is no accident that there are twenty-six "circuit" chapters in this book (twenty in section 2 pertaining to teaching children happiness and six in section 3 pertaining to working on our own parental happiness). An electrical circuit is a path or line through which an electrical current flows. Without circuits, we simply cannot power on a light, and similarly without these tools, we cannot reliably power on our children's lights at the beginning of the tunnel. Think of the circuit breaker panel that is found in every home: It works to distribute electricity to specific areas of your home, and that is the image I want you to think of here. With every chapter topic that we successfully wire within our children and ourselves, we are filling that cognitive circuit board that will enable the light of happiness to flow stronger to every part of ourselves and our families.

While you can take as much time as you need to work on mastering each topic individually with your children, I challenge you to add a new skill to your repertoire every two weeks, so that by the end of one year (fifty-two weeks) you have completed the installation of all basic components of the happiness circuits in this book (twenty-six circuits).

Now for some troubleshooting. Even if you find yourself only having the time, focus, and practical headspace to incorporate some of these circuits, that is fine as well. Realize the power of every marginal improvement you can give your children. To illustrate this, I want to tell you the story of the British Team Sky professional cycling team. Team

Sky was one of the worst national cycling teams, to the point where manufacturers were beginning to refuse to sell them new bikes in fear of having their company name seen on products ridden by this team. Sporting guru Sir Dave Brailsford was hired in 2003 to try to improve them, and he took a unique approach. Instead of trying to overhaul their system, he looked for all the little, marginal things he could do to give them an edge, which, when combined, added up to some big net gains. He took into account tire pressure, helmet air resistance, post-race massage-gels, and even the pillows they were using at night. He investigated ways for them to eat and sleep optimally. And by making all these small improvements, he managed to transform his rag-tag team into what many consider one of the best sports teams in the world, winning three of the world's most difficult and prestigious bike races (the Tour de France) in four years. And so, never underestimate the power of small changes, especially when grouped together as many small changes over time. Imagine how much brighter your home could be in just one year!

I hope this compilation of some of the most popular and profound happiness research and techniques will serve as a lifeboat. My blessing to you is that you will find several *avanim tovos* floating toward you in this book, that will help both you and your children illuminate what is important as you wade through the choppy waters of parenting.

CHAPTER 1

Why Are Today's Children Unhappy?

Happiness has become a scientific pursuit in our generation. Over the past decade, I have been inundated with advertisements to attend courses on happiness (I must admit that I finally gave in to one), received books on happiness as gifts, and had dinners with friends where most of their conversation revolved around "happiness projects" and ways they were trying to teach themselves to be happy. While all this seems great, I think the happiness craze has overlooked the most important part of the population; this is what needs to be examined if we are ever going to combat the tendency toward unhappiness in our modern society in a more permanent way. We are focused on enlightening ourselves, but we are still stuck in the mentality that our children will somehow come upon happiness naturally. Chalk it up to idealism, over-reliance on the innocence of youth, or even just the desperate hope that we are giving our children the most privileged childhoods of any generation, so hey—what do they have to complain about? But the reality is that children today are also missing the boat on the best mental attitudes. As a fellow parent recently described, "My child has everything he needs, but all he can focus on is how he doesn't have the trading cards he wants."

According to the American Psychological Organization, in their report "Consumerism and its Discontents" by Tori DeAngelis, the average American, compared to Americans in 1957, has twice as many cars per person, eats at restaurants twice as much, and of course enjoys endless devices to simplify their lives. Israel and other nations around the world are enjoying similar statistics. And yet, according to Hope College Professor David G. Myers, today's young adults are growing up with less happiness and much greater risk of depression and assorted social pathology in tandem.[1] Why?

I believe the answer is that there are unique challenges that come with abundance, just like there are unique challenges that come with deprivation. *Chazal* back this up in many places as well.[2] But what are we doing about this? Are we educating our youth and equipping them with life skills to address and combat these challenges, or are we still sticking our heads in the sand and pretending that happiness is something that "should just come naturally"?

In a June 2009 New York Times article directed at high school graduates, David Brooks points out that at least formally, we are definitely employing the ostrich approach. He describes society as a mess (his own words). "It is structured to distract people from the decisions that have a huge impact on happiness in order to focus attention on [other] decisions." He cites the abundance of courses and guidance that are offered to young adults on the decision of where to go to college and find a career, while at the same time, there is no formal training for how to select a spouse, no curriculum to teach the talent of making and keeping friends, and no classes on how to control one's impulses—all life skills that have been shown to be inextricably tied to one's happiness.

Positive psychology has emerged as a powerhouse of the twenty-first century: researching the topic, providing empirical proofs for its methods, and disseminating its knowledge to the adult masses. But what of our younger children? Why wait until they reach their older years and realize they are unhappy and need to "undo" their unhappiness? Visiting Israeli professor Tal Ben Shahar's Harvard positive psychology class exploded from twenty students to 850 students within a few years, as some of the most brilliant, well-equipped, and privileged students from around the world clamored to find skills to combat their unhappiness.

---

1   https://bit.ly/3k6Iicj; https://bit.ly/2BQhVWS.
2   *Mesilas Yesharim*, ch. 1.

The bottom line is that we need to start cultivating more positivity, gratitude, and optimism in our children, and teach them the tools to glean real happiness from the world around them. Happiness training should be on the short list of life-skill training essentials, right up there with riding a bike, swimming, and self-defense. After all, why should the aforementioned be more of a milestone than learning how to live a happy life?

Our children are ready for it, too. Go out and see what fascinates these young minds and notice that they are already looking past the mundane side of life: Mystery, magic, and miracles capture their imaginations (and ours too, for that matter). Rabbi Shimshon Raphael Hirsch explains that part of our draw toward looking beyond natural phenomenon to the hidden aspect of things was placed in us from the time of our creation. It is meant to lead us to look toward God, who directs and controls all hidden forces. He cites *Koheles* (3:11): "God Has arranged all things beautifully in relation to one another, but He has also put in man's heart a touch of the hidden, of the transcendent..." Our children are searching for something deeper, waiting for us to explain the world to them and make sense of it all. It is up to us to shape their reality and provide them with the necessary life skills even at a young age.

Happiness needs to be actively taught. As an example, upon his return home from his stint at Harvard, Dr. Ben Shahar instituted a program focusing on happiness, morality, and success within certain Israeli schools. In the program, the language of positive psychology became an integral part of school culture. The results Dr. Ben Shahar found included higher GPAs and diminished rates of anxiety, depression, and violence, among others.[3]

We create our children's realities. The question is, how can we actively work to select and form those realities rather than letting them happen on their own? I believe the answer can be uncovered through understanding Judaism's secrets to happiness, wisdom which overlaps considerably with positive psychology. These are the insights that we must

---

3   https://bit.ly/35m8ZFg.

literally plant in our children from a young age: We must teach them to resist the natural urge to compare their lives to others. We must teach them tools for resiliency, mindfulness, deep-seated gratitude, the power of perspective, purpose, positivity, self-acceptance, and so much more.

This book intends to address these and many other issues one by one, or to use our illumination analogy above, circuit by circuit. These circuits will serve as a springboard of ideas and connections on how to proactively work on these life skills with our children, all the while powering up sources of light in our own lives as well.

CHAPTER 2

Who Are My Children?

Do you ever wish your child came with an instruction manual? (And maybe sometimes a pause button?) One might argue that given the sheer volume of parenting books out there, perhaps we should just call those our "manuals." The problem is that we would never read a general book about software to figure out how to use our particular computer, phone, or even vacuum cleaner. We would want the exact manual for our particular make and model! The same reasoning applies for our children, even within the same family; an approach that works for one child often doesn't work for another. In other words, each child is so different that each one needs their own set of instructions to help us raise them optimally. The only problem is that we aren't issued those manuals (although it would certainly be a five-star divine baby shower present if we were).

The good news is that the first thing we will do in this section is explore some of the important features of the "model" you got. In the words of Paul Tournier, "It is quite clear that between love and understanding there is a very close link. He who loves, understands; and he who understands, loves. One who feels understood feels loved, and one who feels loved feels sure of being understood." Even better, by understanding our children on a deeper level, not only will they feel more loved; we will also be on track for figuring out a targeted approach to helping them individually.

Judaism's approach to child-rearing is a big proponent of this specialization—in fact, according to Shlomo HaMelech, this is the starting point of good pedagogy. As he writes in *Mishlei* (22:6): "חֲנֹךְ לַנַּעַר עַל פִּי דַרְכּוֹ‎—Teach a child according to *his* or *her* particular way." The education has to be specialized. And so, to help our children on their own destined path, we need to serve as their first spotlights, illuminating and interpreting their individual road signs, so to speak.

Additionally, the Vilna Gaon teaches that there's a distinction between learned behaviors and natural *middos* (character traits). While part of personal growth is breaking bad behaviors we have learned, another part is identifying the fixed parts of ourselves that don't change and figuring out how to maximize those in our service of God.

Let's start with an exercise to understand our children (and really anyone) better. According to multiple sources, the average amount of decisions a person makes each day ranges from three thousand for a young child, building up to approximately thirty-five thousand as an adult. What this means is that who we really are is a mixture of decisions that lead to action. Therefore, it stands to reason that one of the most powerful things we can do to understand someone is to identify the main forces that drive their decision-making processes. The term I have coined for these forces is "Pilot Light Motivations." Just like a pilot light is always simmering below the surface of a stove, ready to ignite when faced with gas or fuel, so too Pilot Light Motivations represent the driving forces simmering below the surface of every human being's consciousness, ready to ignite when faced with a decision.

First, let's look internally. Ask yourself, what are the emotions that drive most of your decision-making? In my research developing this idea, it was amazing to see the answers people came up with to this exercise. After digging deeply, people responded with motivations like duty, self-consciousness, guilt, expansiveness, anger, laziness, pleasure-seeking, fear, anxiety, and love. There are many more out there. Take some time to write your thoughts on your own Pilot Light Motivations here:

_____

_____

_____

This exercise is not only helpful for self-knowledge but also for action. For example, if we have a motivation that doesn't serve us well in many decision areas (e.g., fear, anxiety, guilt), we can begin to catch ourselves making a choice out of those motivations. Once we are able to see beyond them, we will be able to start shifting to decisions that are more in line with healthy motivations.

It is important to not push hard against these negative motivations that pop up and be upset that they are our motivations to begin with. Our first impulse can often be to control our negative emotions as soon as they surface, so that we don't feel overwhelmed or threatened by them. However, often these negative emotions merit deeper understanding, and running away from them or not letting them calmly run their course can makes things worse. After all, it is difficult to quickly control a strong negative emotion; the more we push it down or try to ignore or repress it, the more it becomes agitated and breaks free.

I heard the following analogy that I think powerfully sums up this issue visually: Imagine that a strong negative emotion is like mud clouding up the waters inside a beautiful fish aquarium. You want to clear the water so you can see the fish and are trying to figure out how to do this. The last thing you want to do is submerge your hands and try to swat at the mud in an attempt to push it to the bottom. After all, the more you try to push it down, the more you churn it up. Similarly, in an attempt to control a negative emotion, you may try to push it down. But the harder you try, the more it resurfaces, swirling around you and muddying your view of a situation or individual.

So, what can we do instead to quiet down those negative Pilot Light Motivations? The answer is to act more like an observer of our emotions rather than the judge, jury, and "disappointment club" (the decidedly opposite of a fan club) when encountering negative emotions. Instead of instantly saying, "I'm furious," "I'm afraid," or "I'm overwhelmed," try to stand back and witness the feelings that are stirring up inside of you without those labels. Know that the negative emotion is only temporary, and is more likely to change with acceptance than with resistance.

Without fueling negative feelings and muddying up the waters, they often ride out the waves and drift off on their own. We are the stories we tell ourselves. Let us not unnecessarily turn them into dramas. We can feel negative but let that feeling dissipate without empowering it to be the driving force behind our decisions in the heat of the moment.

Before we turn to doing this same exercise to uncover our children's Pilot Light Motivations, let's discuss an example that underscores the importance of taking time to identify them. We will examine a situation in which four different children all decide not to do their homework one night. Let's say the skipped assignment was an essay they are required to present to the class about a personal talent. Notice that while the end product of choosing not to do the homework is the same for each child, the driving force behind the decision to not do it could be very different for all four children:

- Child A decides not to do it because one of his Pilot Light Motivations is laziness. It's easier not to do the homework, and he is tired and/or bored after a long day in school. He would much rather play, bother his siblings, or just lie down and read.
- Child B decides not to do it because one of her Pilot Light Motivations is self-consciousness—she is shy and uncomfortable with having to get up in front of the class to present her work. She'd rather push it off and hope that the class runs out of time for presentations before she is forced to do so.
- Child C decides not to do it because one of his Pilot Light Motivations is anger, and he is mad at the teacher (or maybe even his parents) for something that happened that day. This is his way of retaliating.
- Child D decides not to do it because one of her Pilot Light Motivations is pleasure-seeking—she spends too much time on video games or reading that night and gets caught up in entertainment instead of responsibility.

Now let's take some time and write down what the Pilot Light Motivations might be for each of our children, one by one:

_____

_____

_____

_____

_____

_____

Please observe your children through this lens over the next couple weeks and check whether your initial thoughts were correct, or whether you see other motivations spark in them when making a decision that you hadn't initially considered. Again, we are not looking toward the end product of the actual decision; we are analyzing what led them there.

This first exercise should help us dig deeper to figure out what is driving our children. Once we stop focusing on the end product of their decisions, but rather the motivations that led them there, we can get to the root of helping them in a more tailored way.

Now that we understand some of the driving forces behind our children, let us widen the lens to look more at the panorama of their personalities. We need to understand the particular strengths that our children were imbued with, as well as the ways these same strengths can also be sources of weaknesses. Many years ago, Dr. Miriam Adahan put out a gem of a book called *Awareness*. The book presented an ancient system for personality typing known as the Enneagram, adapting it for the Jewish audience. The following chart is an abridged version of the one from *Awareness*.[1]

_____

1   Printed with the permission of Dr. Adahan.

Personality Type	Ideal Level	Intermediate Level	Unhealthy Level
One	Principled, reasonable, objective, tolerant, modest, thrifty, honest, self-disciplined	Strict, impersonal, self-righteous, over-controlling, rule-bound	Punitive, intolerant, perfectionistic, stingy, obsessive-compulsive, contemptuous
Two	Loving, unselfish, humble, protective, empathetic, generous	Approval-seeking, over-extending, possessive, people-pleasing, self-important	Self-centered, guilt-inducing, manipulative, self-deceptive, histrionic
Three	Modest, hard-working, self-assured, intelligent, energetic, resourceful, motivating	Competitive, social-climbing, self-absorbed, elitist, cold, empty, contemptuous	Selfish, arrogant, vain, vindictive, deceptive, exhibitionistic, superficial, amoral
Four	Creative, self-aware, inspiring, gentle, warm, responsible, punctual, genuine, kind	Melancholic, introverted, hypersensitive, elitist, self-pitying	Lonely, undisciplined, irresponsible, self-conscious, self-hating, self-destructive
Five	Intelligent, perceptive, intellectually curious, innovative, scholarly, inspiring, original	Preoccupied, high-strung, absent-minded, aloof, indecisive, speculative, pessimistic, eccentric	Isolated, paranoid, miserly, scornful, autistic, schizophrenic
Six	Trustworthy, committed, faithful, independent, endearing, principled, courageous	Anxious, argumentative, passive-aggressive, suspicious, indecisive, self-doubting, dependent	Phobic, paranoid, hyper-sensitive, self-disparaging, aggressive, controlling, sadistic

Personality Type	Ideal Level	Intermediate Level	Unhealthy Level
Seven	Enthusiastic, resilient, accomplished, optimistic, adventuresome, practical, disciplined, sensitive	Impulsive, charming, uninhibited, worldly, compulsive, addictive, shallow, sybaritic	Pleasure-seeking, glutinous, self-indulgent, narcissistic, insensitive, unmotivated, vulgar, depraved
Eight	Protective, disciplined, courageous, assertive, self-sufficient, humble, productive, innovative	Aggressive, domineering, contemptuous, unemotional, explosive, cunning, adversarial, suspicious	Sadistic, megalomaniacal, ruthless, violent, cruel, sociopathic
Nine	Tranquil, self-possessed, receptive, trusting, tolerant, gentle, self-effacing, calm	Procrastinating, overly-accommodating, easygoing, neglectful, lethargic	Dissociated, repressed, oblivious, fatalistic, passive, unreliable, dependent, numb

As we can see, each personality type has an ideal, intermediate, and unhealthy level of functioning. According to Dr. Adahan, ten percent of the population are functioning at an ideal level, eighty percent at an intermediate level, and ten percent at an unhealthy level.[2] One person can concurrently have a mixture of different traits functioning on different levels within the continuum. Those at the intermediate level can go upscale or downscale depending on their choices at any given moment. For any personality to go upscale, Dr. Adahan recommends choosing and working on: love, humility, respect, positivity, creativity, compassion, self-control, honesty, patience, orderliness, empathy, courage, and determination. As she says quite beautifully, we will know

---

2   Miriam Adahan, *Awareness: The Key to Acceptance, Forgiveness and Growth* (Jerusalem: Feldheim, 1994).

that we are moving upscale when we feel an "ever-increasing awareness of the godliness within people, within yourself and within the world."

What is so nice about the Enneagram is that we see how the same driving forces can produce good or bad expressions, which means that *we can change,* and *our children can change.* If we see a "bad *middah*" in them now, it doesn't mean that they can't change it into a positive one or that this character trait will be manifesting that same way forever. I'd also like to specifically point out how our strengths and weakness are often connected, and can even be two sides of the same coin. Melinda Gates is quoted, in a fascinating *New York Times* article that touched on this topic, as saying, "If one of your strengths is openness, remember that there's a fine line between sharing and oversharing. If you have a flair for moxie and chutzpah, watch out for moments when you're imposing on others. And if you're a spellbinding storyteller, you need to ask whether a dinner party is the ideal time to perform."[3] The keys to a trait manifesting in a positive way are time, place, and degree, all three of which will come into play within section 2.

Now please take a few minutes to look back through the enneagram and try to identify which personality type represents each of your children. If you are having trouble finalizing between two or three types that is perfectly normal. Also, do not worry if one or two traits within an otherwise-fitting personality type description seem totally off for your child; we are not trying to put each person in a box, but find general trends that go along with each child's personality in order to understand each one better.

_____

_____

_____

_____

---

3   https://nyti.ms/32diCUI.

Consider the following example that should help you narrow down the personality types further: A group of children are all in the middle of a school outing to a trampoline facility, and each one has the following thoughts:

- **Type 1**: "Jumping on these trampolines is so ridiculous. I'd rather be at home reading."
- **Type 2**: "Almost everyone seems to be having fun except Rochel over there in the corner. I'll go hang out with her to make her feel better."
- **Type 3**: "As I look around, I see that I am wearing the prettiest dress and am the best jumper."
- **Type 4**: "I feel so alone. If only I could find one friend to hang around with and then talk to on the bus ride home, I'd have a much better time."
- **Type 5**: "I hate having to come to these outings and be with all these people, I'd rather be at home working on my robot set or at school learning something in class."
- **Type 6**: "I was on the student council committee that planned this school outing—if the other kids don't enjoy it, they'll all blame me. But it's not my fault, I did my best!"
- **Type 7**: "I love it here, what fun! I wish we could come jumping on trampolines every day."
- **Type 8**: "This is so disorganized and so many people are bumping into each other. I'd better take charge by making a line, and saying when the next person can jump in."
- **Type 9**: "How nice, everyone is having so much fun together and getting along. This is how it should be every day whether we are in school or on an outing."

Once we have identified a person's personality type, we can understand many things about them, from their ego fixations to their virtues. Please see the following chart for several insights.[4]

---

4   Primarily adapted from Don Richard Riso and Russ Hudson, *Understanding the Enneagram: The Practical Guide to Personality Types* (Houghton Mifflin Harcourt, 2000).

Type	Characteristic Role	Ego Fixation	Elevated Idea	Basic Fear	Basic Desire	Temptation	Vice/Passion	Virtue
1	Reformer, Perfectionist	Resentment	Perfection	Corruptness, imbalance, being bad	Goodness, integrity, balance	Hypocrisy, hypercriticism	Anger	Serenity
2	Helper, Giver	Flattery (ingratiation)	Freedom, will	Being unloved	To feel love	Deny own needs, manipulation	Pride	Humility
3	Achiever, Performer	Vanity	Hope, law	Worthlessness	To feel valuable	Pushing self to always be "the best"	Deceit	Truthfulness, authenticity
4	Individualist, Romantic	Melancholy (fantasizing)	Origin	Having no identity or significance	To be uniquely themselves	To overuse imagination in search of self	Envy	Equanimity (emotional balance)
5	Investigator, Observer	Stinginess (retention)	Omniscience, transparency	Helplessness, incapability, incompetence	Mastery, understanding	Replacing direct experience with concept	Avarice	Non-attachment

#	Type							
6	Loyalist, Loyal Skeptic	Cowardice (worrying)	Faith	Being without support or guidance	To have support and guidance	Indecision, doubt, seeking reassurance	Fear	Courage
7	Enthusiast, Epicure	Planning (anticipation)	Wisdom, plan	Being unfulfilled, trapped, deprived	To be satisfied and content	Thinking fulfillment is somewhere else	Gluttony	Sobriety
8	Challenger, Protector	Vengeance (objectification)	Truth	Being controlled, harmed, violated	Self-protection	Thinking they are completely self-sufficient	Forcefulness	Innocence
9	Peacemaker, Mediator	Indolence (daydreaming)	Love	Loss, fragmentation, separation	Wholeness, peace of mind	Avoiding conflicts, avoiding self-assertion	Sloth (disengagement)	Action

People can also have contradictory parts or emotions inside of them and this, too, is normal. Bestselling American author Elizabeth Gilbert put it this way: "None of us are really an individual, per se, but rather we are each a teeming multitude of contradictory selves. There are parts of ourselves who are strong, parts of us who are vulnerable, parts of us who are angry, parts of us who are entitled…This is what we mean when we say, 'Part of me is really angry at you right now, even though another part of me completely understands the situation.'"

Therefore, don't be too concerned if you see your children acting in contradictory ways in different situations. If they are normally giving, but a certain type of situation makes their possessive or miserly side come out, this is normal. And if they are usually kind but you find they act mean in certain situations, this can also be normal. We can help them understand how to navigate these situations by figuring out the underlying triggers for their internal contradictory selves.[5]

---

5   For more on this, read Dr. Richard Schwartz's work on internal family systems.

CHAPTER 3

What Is Growth?

But now what? Does this "model" define us forever? Absolutely not. We are not machines, hunks of heartless metal with no ability to adapt. Our humanity comes with the great gift of change, the opportunity for self-improvement—God's glorious gift of growth. We must believe that even our children have the tremendous potential to make this happen. Whether it is improving their traits or just harnessing their powers for the better, we can help them along this path. After all, once we understand where someone is coming from, we can help them get to where they need to go.

The term for a person's character traits in Judaism is *middos*, and we are told that Hebrew words often reflect a deeper meaning at their core. The literal meaning of *middos* is "measurements," which means that the Hebrew language is telling us that by way of these character traits, we can truly measure a person. The *Even Sheleimah* (1:2) says that the main service of God is refining one's *middos* and questions what the deeper purpose of this Divine-given life is if one is *not* working on them? Many of us have growth charts on our walls for our children as they grow taller. Imagine the impact if we had ones available for spiritual and character growth as well. One of the great tenets of Judaism is that no one is ever seen as "stuck" in a bad trait, or even in a bad record of sins. Each person can grow and change who they are at any given time.

The Talmud (*Avodah Zarah* 17a) records several stories of average (or even wicked) individuals who successfully accomplished this. These individuals managed to earn their entire share in the World to Come in one great act. The phrase the Talmud uses for this is "יֵשׁ קוֹנֶה עוֹלָמוֹ בְּשָׁעָה אַחַת,"

25

which is translated as, "There are those who earn their entire share in the World to Come in one moment." However, the *Baal HaTanya* takes a different approach, using the rich nuanced meanings of the Hebrew language to interpret *"shaah"* by its other meaning, which is "to turn."[1] Thus, according to the *Baal HaTanya*, the people recorded in these stories earned their shares in the World to Come not because of one hour of good deeds but because of one turn that they made! By making one change to who they were as people, it sent their lives on a completely different trajectory (next stop, *Olam Haba*), much like a guided missile. In other words, if we make one change in our coordinates, we can head down a totally different life path.

God believes so much in our power to change that we are reminded of this at the beginning of each day. The first prayer we are supposed to say when we wake up in the morning is *Modeh Ani*, which translates into English as follows:

> *I offer thanks to You, Living and Eternal King, for You have mercifully restored my soul within me; Your faithfulness is great.*

The famous question on this is, what is the "faith" that we are *thanking God* for in having given back our souls? Aren't we the only ones that need faith? The answer is that God's faith in us is the faith that we can still change, that we can grow, that we can reach the potential that our souls were put here for—no matter what we did to these souls yesterday to muddle their mission or set them off course. The *Chasam Sofer* adds that if God has given our *neshamos* (souls) back, it means that He believes in our abilities *today*, and we must have this same faith in our children's growth potential.

There has been a lot of research on the type of people who are more hardwired for growth, and Carol Dweck is probably the most famous name in that field. She developed what she calls the tenets of the "growth mindset," which reflects which people and children are most

---

1   As in the story of Kayin and Hevel, when the Torah says, "אֶל־מִנְחָתוֹ לֹא שָׁעָה—God did not turn to his offering" (*Bereishis* 4:5).

primed for growth. I'd like to highlight the following from her book on the topic.

Dweck's philosophy is that our growth should follow the step-by-step nature of progress. In her research, Dweck gave children a number of tasks with increasing difficulty and found that children with growth mindset didn't say they were "failing" at the hard tasks, but instead framed it in terms of "learning."

From this research she identified two mindsets:

- The first is the *fixed mindset*, which is driven by the belief that people can't really change and that qualities are carved in stone. This creates an urgency to prove oneself. These types of people shy away from challenges because they think their deficiencies will be unmasked. As we can imagine, this significantly narrows their world and their growth potential.
- The second is the *growth mindset*, which is driven by the belief that people can change through their efforts. Learning and effort are critical factors in this process.

Dweck recommends engendering the growth mindset by praising children more widely based on efforts rather than talents and end products. After all, many of us know brilliant people who didn't get very far in life with their natural talents, and not-so-bright people who got very far by putting in the hard work. I believe that the growth mindset pairs very well with the Jewish mindset that growth can always happen, and we should not be afraid to put in work to achieve our goals. The Talmud (*Berachos* 17a) says: "אַשְׁרֵי מִי שֶׁגָּדֵל בַּתּוֹרָה וַעֲמָלוֹ בַּתּוֹרָה, וְעוֹשֶׂה נַחַת רוּחַ לְיוֹצְרוֹ—Praiseworthy is the person who worked hard at learning Torah. This is the person who gives pride and joy to His Creator." We should teach our children to not be afraid to work hard and never give up on their ability to reach their goals.

CHAPTER 4

What Is Happiness?

Well, the answer to that question depends. Happiness is a talent of sorts, and just like some people have more raw talent in some areas than others, some people have more raw happiness skills than others. What comes out of this is that just like talents can be developed when consistently worked on, so too anyone can become a happiness virtuoso with proper practice.

Some of us also might find it easier to answer what happiness is *not*, rather than what it is. The reason this seemingly simple question is so challenging to answer is because happiness is really a bit different for everyone, almost like a precision instrument that needs to be calibrated for the user. And therefore, it is imperative for each person to learn what they need; not at an external level, like balloons and lollipops, but on a deeply internal level, such as learning to honor our truest selves.

Susan David, author of *Emotional Agility*, writes: "To be truly happy...one must know simply how to 'be,' and by that, I mean to be effectively with oneself—centered, kind, curious and not fragile—in a changing world." Carol Tuttle drives this point home further in her book *The Child Whisperer* when she writes: "[C]onsider how many high-performing, depressed adults we already have in this world. They know how to do, do, do—but do they know how to just *be*?"

Psychological constructionists emphasize that we are always in some state of core emotion, which affects our viewing, interpreting, and interacting with the daily flow of events around us. Feelings are explained as blends of pleasure-displeasure and activation-deactivation. Because we have multiple things going on in our lives at any given moment, it stands to reason that we are really experiencing many different feelings at once. Unless it's your wedding day, you are probably not "all happy." And for many, even on their wedding day, there are other feelings that blend in as well (sadness about the relative that couldn't be at the wedding, anxiety related to starting a new stage of life, or even fear of something going wrong at the wedding itself after all the careful planning). Therefore, because our feelings are blends, most emotions are not truly "pure" such as "all happy" or "all upset." If you were to graph your emotions, you would see how you are really experiencing an emotional state that has no real label at any given moment. An example of this is the following emotion "circumplex structure," created by Dr. James Russel with the vertical axis representing the degree of activation-deactivation and the horizontal axis representing the degree of pleasure-displeasure.[1]

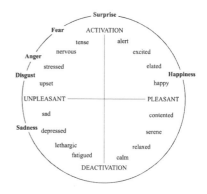

This shows us how complex it is to really define "happiness" and to understand that there is a range within the emotion. Often, we have achieved a level of the "happiness" definition without even knowing it, such as when we are feeling just "calm" or "relaxed." Personally, it helped me a lot to recognize that happiness has many different shades, and just because I don't feel giddy or elated most of the time doesn't mean I am unhappy.

In terms of real unhappiness, most people are unhappy when they don't feel they are in touch with their real selves and their abilities; when they are trying to be someone they are not, or are doing something they're not really good at or meant to excel at. Reflect for a moment on the following questions:

- Do my children know who they are and accept themselves?
- Do I really feel *I* know who my children are and do *I* accept them?

1   James A. Russell, "A Circumplex Model of Affect," *Journal of Personality and Social Psychology*, 39, 6 (1980): 1161–1178.

- Are they busy trying to be someone that they are not (or am I trying to make them someone that they are not)?

Tuttle also asks parents to reflect on the question, "Are the things that I make big deals out of really important in the big picture for them or at their developmental stage?" There is a related concept that comes up in the story of Yishmael, probably the first child in the Torah to ever be called out by an adult for bad behavior. In the story in *Bereishis*,[2] Sarah gets Avraham to kick Yishmael out of the house because, as *Chazal* tell us, she sees his bad behavior and is able to foresee how this will lead to even worse behavior in the future. Hashem tells Hagar that He is going to heed Yishmael's cry and save him because of "בַּאֲשֶׁר הוּא שָׁם," which according to *Rashi* means where he is in life at the moment. The Talmud (*Rosh Hashanah* 16b) elaborates on this to say that even though the angels were accusing Yishmael based on terrible things that they knew would come out of him in the future, God stood firm in only judging him based on the present moment.

---

2   Ch. 21.

CHAPTER 5

How Should We View
Our Children?

The idea brought out by the story of Yishmael is that everyone needs to be judged for the stage and level they are at *right now*. What makes this concept difficult for many parents is that when they see bad behavior in their child, they are not able to stay in the

MINDSET MALFUNCTION mental moment. The higher standards that we demand for our children, often in non-age-appropriate ways, come from our minds running away with us and thinking decades ahead to how this is going to play out if our child continues this or that undesirable behavior. Imagination can wreak havoc on our lives. Comfort yourself in knowing that most issues resolve themselves with time, as children mature after a few years (or for some when they reach adulthood). Pushing them to be someone they are not at any given stage is usually counterproductive.

Consider the following thoughts and their mental time travel:

- "If he has such separation anxiety now when I leave him at nursery school, how is he ever going to function as an adult?" (Spoiler alert: He is not going to be clinging and crying to take him home when you walk him down to the *chuppah*.)
- "If she can't organize herself now, will she ever be able to hold down a job and run a household?" (Spoiler alert: She can indeed find ways to run a beautiful household, even if she is messier than her neighbors or it is not how you would personally do it.)

- "If he hits his siblings so much now, doesn't this mean he is going to be an aggressive adult? Is he going to be a cruel husband?" (Spoiler alert: Some of the nicest people I know now acted out with age-appropriate aggression when they were younger.)

When you look at your children, try to remove your time-travel glasses and replace them with your "בַּאֲשֶׁר הוּא שָׁם" glasses—look at them right now, with their chubby hands, crooked smiles, and childhood whimsy in their eyes and try to truly *see them* in this moment. True love is the blessing of knowing and being known. That is why giving full attention to our children and looking them in the eyes when we talk to them is so important—it is showing we care who they are, and that we want to fully engage with them and get to know them *in this moment.*

This is not to say that we shouldn't try to improve their behavior or act on improving serious shortcomings. It is merely reminding us that many things will work themselves out with maturity, and we have to be able to distinguish between normal age-appropriate misdeeds and red flags. And we can always consult a professional if we are not sure.

Which brings me to the next confounding variable that is important to keep in mind when we feel triggered by our children's behavior. Many things we judge our children for have very little to do with them. Instead, they have much to do with both our *projections* into *their* futures and, for lack of a better term, *rejections* into *our* own pasts. We want matters to play out for our children a certain way, want them to take the path we wish we had for ourselves if only we had done things differently. And so, before you fight with your child, ask yourself, "Is this about me or is this about my child?" It's a powerful question, one that can really rip you out of the mental time travel that causes so much unnecessary *hakpadah* (exactitude) and strife.

Which leads me to the giant plot twist, right here at the beginning of the book, no less! At the end of the day, the goal for our children is not actually happiness in and of itself. Happiness is a hot topic and buzzword of our times, but what we are really seeking for our children as we set them off on the dusty gravel path of adulthood, is to be *well-adjusted*. Happiness is part of this, but as we noted above, even that emotion feels different for various people. There are many people who fall in different parts of the emotion circumplex structure above that are "content" but wouldn't necessarily describe themselves as "elated." There are plenty of serious, simple folks that might not walk around with giant smiles but are at peace inside. All of these skills that we are discussing are to aid you in helping your children adjust to this world: to maximize childhood growth potential in order to create growth-minded/growth-ready adults; to give over emotional agility—that GPS that helps us recalculate our lives to find peace, proper mindset, and ultimately redemption; and to build a foundation of solid outlook and proper action that makes our children internally wired for happiness, instead of scrambling to find it in external objects later in life. Let us now take out our tools for wiring our mental circuits, and begin.

Wiring the Circuits

Foundations for Powering on the Light
at the Beginning of the Tunnel

Mind

CHAPTER 6

Circuit 1:
The Power of Perspective

*"A person should always [take care] not to cast his
thoughts backward [to the past], for his eyes are
placed on his face and not his back."*

Letters of the Rambam 262

"The seeing see little."

Helen Keller

My grandfather felt as if he had been born twice: Once from his
mother's womb and once from underneath a haystack.

During the ravages of World War II, my grandfather found himself
fleeing from a band of Nazis on foot. Out of breath, out of options, and
(even worse) seemingly out of luck, he found himself in a farm field.
The Nazis were approaching, and he quickly buried himself under one
of the countless haystacks in sight. Reaching the field and not seeing
their desired victim, one of the Nazi's picked up a pitchfork and began
stabbing the stacks, suspecting that the target was hidden within one.
It was at that moment that my grandfather considered his life as over.

Many decades later, on his actual deathbed, he revealed this story
for the first time to my father and his sisters. He implored them,
"Don't be sad for me when I die now. Do not think about the years
ahead that I will never live. I made a deal with God from under that

haystack decades ago that if He would extend my life even one day, I would forever be grateful. And look how many moments, days, and years I got...dying now is something to rejoice over." It was in this way that he saw his death as a genuine success. He had lived on borrowed time from the Master of the Universe for decades, seen children and grandchildren, and been granted a new life the minute he heard the pitchfork tossed away in frustration after all the haystacks the Nazis chose to stab were found to be empty. Can you imagine the silence in that field as the Nazis stomped away? It was in that silence that my grandfather was reborn.

I was thirteen years old when my beloved grandfather passed away and the story from his deathbed has clung to me ever since, like remaining bits of hay that can't seem to be shaken off. It taught me the incredible tool of perspective; namely, that we actually choose what we see. Just like the same piece of art can be displayed in front of a group of people and each one will see something different in it, so too is life. After all, life is the ultimate artistic masterpiece, and a group of people can have the same experiences and yet all see them and react differently. This is an invaluable lesson to actively teach our children: They actually have the power to choose how they see situations and how they react to them. Life is not a stimulus and we the passive responders—we are all active responders, and whether or not we think we are actively choosing our perspective, we actually do precisely that every single moment.

The Torah shows us this message, right from the first story of Gan Eden. In that archetypical paradise, Adam and Chavah had very little in terms of personal possessions, and yet they had everything they could possibly need. Focusing on what they lacked rather than the amazing paradise at their fingertips ruined everything. Thinking of the unattainable fruit made them suddenly feel that they were missing out, when in reality, God had created a gorgeous garden where they lacked nothing of necessity. This first man and woman had enough to focus on and enjoy for a lifetime. To make matters worse, Rabbinic tradition teaches that they didn't even last one day—by nightfall of the first day in Gan Eden they already declared their glasses as half-empty, they had eaten the fruit, and they were banished from the Garden.[1]

Other Torah examples of the power of perspective abound. The Torah records how Yaakov and Eisav, during their fateful meeting after a long separation, update each other on decades of their lives apart. Eisav describes his worldly lot as "יֶשׁ לִי רָב—I have **most** of what I need,"[2] while Yaakov describes his lot as "יֶשׁ לִי כֹל—I have **everything** I could possibly need."[3] It wasn't that one had objectively so much more than the other—they just had different perspectives on their lives.

I try to talk to my children about this concept, and help them challenge their negative perspectives whenever they bubble to the surface (unfortunately, more often than I would like):

- "I'm bored, Mommy, there's nothing to do." *"Is it really true that there is nothing to do? Can you name me five things that would be possible to do in this room?"*
- "I never get to have the first turn!" *"Is that really true? Or are you only remembering the times when you didn't get the first turn? Can we think of times in this past week where you actually did have the first turn?"*

MINDSET MALFUNCTION

Children are very prone to black and white—or also aptly termed, "all-or-nothing"—thinking. Statements about always and forever are some of their main "go-to's" and it's important to gently guide them out of this habit. When they tell us, "You never let me stay up late" or "I will be small forever," we should gently point out how this thinking is flawed. "Can you think of all the special occasions you've stayed up late for this year?" or "Did you know that I used to feel like I'd be small forever too? Now look how tall I grew, but it took time."

All-or-nothing thinking tends to make people feel hopeless and sad, so it is imperative to steer our children away from this flawed perspective as early as possible. And while you are at it, don't forget to watch and catch your own all-or-nothing statements. Saying things like, "You

---

1   *Midrash Shocher Tov* on *Tehillim*.
2   *Bereishis* 33:9.
3   Ibid., 33:11.

never listen to me," or "You are always hitting your sister," only teaches children to exaggerate and say things in the language of extremes as well. The truth is they do (hopefully often) listen to us, and there *are* of course plenty of activities in their lives that don't involve picking on a particular sibling.

In the words of Helen Keller, "The seeing see little." It's all about perspective in life, and we need to both model and teach how shifting our view of situations can literally shift us from sadness to happiness (or at least acceptance, which we will be exploring in depth later). Sometimes, when we close our eyes and actively open our minds, we are able to peak through the strands of hay from under the stack and begin to choose how to see things. And that is the moment we too can be reborn as we learn to truly see.

Where to Begin: Takeaways and Tips

📖 Teachable Moments

- Notice when your children use all-or-nothing language. Try to get them to realize this by gently questioning those statements.
- Challenge negative perspectives by asking questions to see whether the negativity is well-founded.
- Help your children see things from other viewpoints in interpersonal situations to broaden their perspectives.

💬 Discussion Starters

- When your children are complaining to you about what they don't have, ask them if they can list several things that they do have before you are willing to listen to the complaint.
- If your children come home telling you only the negative things that happened that day, ask them if they can also list three positive ones (this will force them to become aware of them).

⬛ Reinforcement

Purchase glass beads or something else visually interesting. Give them to your children as "perspective points" when they choose to find something positive in a situation they could have complained about, or successfully see a situation from another person's point of view. They can cash them in for prizes or make a "perspective jar" out of these in the end. To do so, fill a jar with the beads in any order/mix (much like colorful sand), and when they look at the jar from different sides, they will see different patterns!

Circuit 2:
Embracing the Now

"אִם אֲנִי כָּאן הַכֹּל כָּאן"—*If I am here, everything
is here.*"

Statement of Hillel in Talmud, Sukkah 63a

*"Yesterday is history, tomorrow is a mystery, and
today is a gift—that's why we call it the present."*

Origin unknown

Years ago, I was asked to be the keynote speaker at an event that
was scheduled to take place a few hours after I'd be flying home from
a trip. I happily agreed, put down the phone, and promptly proceeded
to get nervous. What if the plane was delayed? What if my kids didn't
sleep well on the trip all crammed together on back-to-back air mat-
tresses, woke us up throughout the night, and thus generously shared
the sleep deprivation? What if I couldn't rub two brain cells together to
offer up a coherent sentence after a day of family cross-country travel?
Instantly, my mind was off to the races even though the trip was an
entire month away.

Thankfully, I was able to bring myself back to the present moment by
realizing that either I could be thinking about all these remote, unlikely
factors (*and had I considered the possibility that a meteor might strike the
earth?*) or I could go about enjoying my life for the next month, have

fun on the trip, and then go ahead and let all my nerves run wild during that one hour before the speech. By then I'd have a better sense of what had actually played out leading up to that hour anyway. Thank God, I was able to do the latter and everything fell into place, the speaking engagement worked out wonderfully, and even the meteor decided not to head our way.

The tool I employed here is one of the gems behind the cognitive behavioral therapy approach that has become a powerhouse in psychology over the last few decades. Known as "mindfulness," it is the ability to not let sadness, fears, or even recurring thoughts ruin the present moment. After all, reasons for anxiety often exist in the past or the future, but rarely in the exact moment in which a person is presently living. In other words, anxiety mainly comes from being upset over something that happened in the past or from being afraid of something that might happen in the future, while the here-and-now moment is usually quite peaceful and often downright enjoyable.

Classic examples include:

- People who leave before the last innings of a baseball game because they are worried about what traffic will be like on the way home from the stadium once the game ends.
- People who can't enjoy a meal out for a special occasion because they are worried about how the children are doing at home with the babysitter or the emails piling up in their inbox while they dine.

MINDSET MALFUNCTION

Take an everyday, commonplace scenario as well: Think about a car drive where you are stressing about a difficult conversation that needs to be had with your boss once you get to work. You are all worked up over what might happen in that future conversation, but meanwhile there is so much serenity you are failing to notice in the current moment: the silence in the car, the cool air rushing through your window, the brilliant sunshine outside, and so much more that would be enjoyable if you would just let yourself focus on the present surroundings. But instead you are trying to preemptively figure out all the things that could go wrong with the future encounter.

The question is, why ruin any other moments that exist outside of that future conversation? The car ride is yours to enjoy—or waste—depending on whether you want to let future cause for anxiety seep into your present chance for peace. The truth is that the more we think of it, most of life is the car ride, and very few moments are the anxiety-provoking-conversation-with-the-boss variety. Life is busy happening while we are worrying about other things. Bringing ourselves back to the present moment whenever we find our minds spiraling out of control can create so much more serenity in the here and now.

The more I learn about mindfulness, the more I see it in Judaism as well. Mindfulness is directly related to *menuchas hanefesh*, and the concept is elaborated upon skillfully by Rabbi Chaim Friedlander in his *sefer, Sifsei Chaim*.[1] Rabbi Friedlander insists that a person's spiritual well-being and *menuchas hanefesh* depend on their ability to be present in a mindful manner. He astutely observes that young people are often frustrated because they are living in the future, and the elderly are similarly stymied by living in the past. The theme of present-ness plays out in mitzvos ranging from prayer (being present before the Almighty) to Shabbos observance (being present in a point in time).

Rabbi Shimshon Raphael Hirsch looks at it from a slightly different vantage point. He states that "people commonly cope with distress by turning their thoughts to the future. By looking to the future, they seek solace for a disconsolate present. Our Sages did the opposite…our Sages taught us to look upon every moment of the present as part of the future…upon everything that happens to us and all that we experience in the present, as part of eternity…for every moment truly lived is of the essence of that eternity which we will all ultimately share and can attain even in this life, if we are what we ought to be."[2] In other words, Rabbi Hirsch underscores the present moment as being the building block of everything. We need to appreciate the present and not just look to the future, because as he beautifully expresses, the present really is the *building block of our future*. Therefore, we ought to be living to the

---

1   Chapter titled "*Menuchas Hanefesh*."
2   Rabbi Shimshon Raphael Hirsch on *Bereishis* 21:33.

fullest now. Mindfulness is a critical tool for our spiritual well-being that directly impacts our general happiness. Only by living in the here and now can we find true joy and peace.

Mindfulness exercises work well for children over age five. Eline Snel, who created the Eline Snel Method for mindfulness training in school-children, says these exercises can help "calm the churning thoughts in their heads, learn to feel and understand their emotions and improve their concentration." She goes on to say that a lot of children nowadays are extremely insecure, thinking they are not good or cool enough when compared with their peers. She warns that some of these children "worry and then deal with their distorted self-image by either with-drawing or drawing attention to themselves, trying to please others or being selfish, or by bullying or acting tough." They can become trapped in these maladaptive behavioral patterns.

I would encourage people to talk to their older children about mind-fulness using its actual term so they have a word to associate with their experiences. When they are stressing out about something in their future (a school test, dating, etc.), encourage them to slow down. Tell them to close their eyes and "listen" to the current moment; stop think-ing about what is bothering them and just breathe, listen to the sound of nature outside, and reflect on how wonderful it feels to be alive right now. Tell them that for the next week, whenever that anxiety-ridden fu-ture topic comes up in their minds, they should do the same refocusing exercise or even pre-pick a topic they would prefer to pull their mind to. This will get them in the habit of refocusing. Examples of a pre-chosen topic could be thoughts of a future vacation, plans with friends for the upcoming Shabbos, excitement for summer camp, etc. Slowly, it will become a habit for them to "inhabit" their present moments instead of being locked out from them by future worries. See section 3 of this book for several powerful mindfulness exercises and activities. These can be incorporated into the family routine.

While it is harder to teach younger children to be mindful, we can introduce certain pieces of mindfulness at a young age and develop these skills as they grow older. Teach them how to be present, and never underestimate the power of distraction to help them learn how to refocus. When disappointments escalate to a tantrum, children often forget, after a few minutes, why they are so upset. And so, if we fall into the trap of trying to talk them out of being upset, positive results are unlikely to happen. Instead of reasoning with them in the heat of their distress, try simply refocusing them on something else in their immediate surroundings. Frequently, they are then able to move past the crying. It could be as simple as, "Hey did you notice how much snow fell outside this morning? Let's go look," or leading them by the hand to the kitchen and saying, "Let's go have some warm apple juice." Refocusing on the moment can be taught even from a very young age.

The question that often comes up is how this is any different than "escapism" (trying to ignore, hide, or run away from reality). With mindfulness, we are not saying that problems don't exist, we are merely saying that the problems don't need to take over our lives and control us at every given moment. Mindfulness allows us to put boundaries in place and not let ourselves dwell or wallow. We are compartmentalizing what gets thought about when, and not letting the past or future ruin our present. We need to teach our children that we can actually have control over our minds and thoughts: We can either rehash something that happened last week (or last month, or even last year) a thousand times, or instead let it be a "one and done." We can be afraid or nervous about something we have to do next week for the entire week leading up to it, or only for the preceding hour or even few minutes before it.

The power we have over our pain and fear is greater than we think, but only if we are able to harness our minds and not let our minds harness us. And so, as we teach our children to embrace this mysterious gift known as the present, may they merit to handle it with care and truly *live*.

Where to Begin: Takeaways and Tips

▣ Discussion Starters

First, talk to your children about how to be present in the current moment.

✗ Tools

- Use distraction when necessary to help them learn how to get unstuck from the previous thought and to refocus.
- Get a book on mindfulness activities and try incorporating them into the family routine.
- Try simple breathing exercises with your children as well. For example:
  - Breathe in for four counts through your nose, breathe out for four counts through your mouth.
  - Tell them to put one hand on their chest and one on their stomach and feel their body rise and fall as you count breaths for them, in and out.

▥ Teachable Moment

When you catch your child upset/ruminating about a situation that is not currently at hand, do a simple breathing exercise or a five senses exercise to bring them into the current moment:

- What is the smallest sound you hear right now and the loudest sound? What is the furthest thing you see and the closest? What are some smells you can sense right now?

CHAPTER 8

Circuit 3:
The Fading Art of Patience

*"A person should always be patient like Hillel and
not exacting like Shammai."*

Talmud, Shabbos 30b

*"Patience is not the ability to wait, but the ability
to keep a good attitude while waiting."*

Anonymous

In the Torah, there is an interesting term describing the pain that Moshe saw the Jews enduring amid their slavery in Egypt: "וַיַּרְא בְּסִבְלֹתָם—He saw their suffering."[1] The interesting aspect of the term סבלתם comes from its root, סבל, which is actually shared with the Hebrew word for patience, סבלנות. The fact that patience and suffering have the same root in the Hebrew language speaks volumes about the emotions many of us go through when we are left hanging or waiting.

But why is this? Why is it so hard to have patience and what is so uncomfortable about needing to wait? In essence, waiting is a very passive action, and yet suffering seems at its core to be a very active experience. The two don't seem to fit.

---

1   *Shemos* 2:11.

Someone recently posited to me that impatience results from feeling like there is disorder in the world when there should be order. For example:

- "Why is this line so long? This store should really have more cashiers..."
- "Why is my plane delayed? This airport/airline should be more on top of prompt departures..."
- "Why is it taking so long to find a spouse? I see so many people around me finding their *bashert* so easily..."

We experience pain during the process of impatience because we feel the pressure of something we want to control moving totally out of our control. I believe that the antidote to this problem can be summed up in the famous phrase, "Let go and let God." Everything is for a reason, even waiting in a long line at a grocery store. We may not realize it at the moment (or may never realize it), but when we are stuck waiting, there really is a reason that we are going through that experience.

Whether they were waiting for something big like meeting their spouse or something small like catching their bus, there are countless examples of people who can report compelling reasons in hindsight why it was better for them to have waited. In some cases, people realize they hadn't been properly equipped yet for the thing they were waiting for; in some cases, the fact that they waited even kept them safe from an impending disaster. There are countless stories of people who were delayed getting to work at the World Trade Center on 9/11, and those delays ended up saving their lives. In another amazing occurrence, my husband's chronically late *chavrusa* mentioned that his chronically late namesake was (shocking, I know) late for catching his spot on the *Titanic*. In this story, his life was literally saved by "missing the boat"! In all these cases, hindsight revealed that what seemed like upending annoyance actually prevented impending disaster.

We should teach our children to entertain the idea that simpler benefits from waiting exist as well: It could be that waiting gave them some extra time to think and they had a novel idea or came up with a solution to a problem they had been struggling with. Or it could just be that waiting gave them time to smile at someone in line who was having a terrible day and needed that moment of cheer.

If we teach our children that there actually *is* order in the world, even in mundane situations, they will habitually learn the skills to calm themselves down in the not-so-mundane situations too. When we realize that a situation requiring patience is the order set out for us right now, we will recognize in the moment that things haven't gone as we've wanted them to for a reason. The biggest shift we can make to help children with their patience is to teach them to accept that *they* can't change a situation, but they can change *themselves* in the situation.

Patience requires waiting for what you want, and thus, a large piece of this also has to do with teaching our children how to deal with delayed gratification. This is important because according to the *Meshech Chochmah* (*Devarim* 6:5), the ability to accept delayed gratification is what separates man from animals. In the late 1960s, psychologist Walter Mischel did a series of studies where he offered children a certain reward that they could get right now (for example a marshmallow) versus an even greater reward if they waited a small amount of time (two marshmallows). Mischel found that children who mustered the self-control to resist eating a marshmallow right away in return for two marshmallows later on, did better in school and were more successful as adults.

Part of teaching over the benefits of having patience and accepting delayed gratification is to explain that almost everything worthwhile takes work, but often the reward is greater when we work harder. Not to mention that when we have to wait for something, it feels better when we finally get it.

Statistics show that the average office worker checks their personal email for 143 minutes each day and typical American mobile users check their phones more than ninety-six times a day, which is twenty percent more, on average, than a few years ago.[2] We are becoming a society that wants everything now, and we need to change this tidal wave tendency with our children before they get lost in the sea of impatience. As we raise our children, we have a tremendous opportunity to help them work on their patience and view delayed gratification in such a way that their סבלנות will not equal סְבְלֹתָם.

Where to Begin: Takeaways and Tips

💬 Discussion Starters

- Ask your children why they think waiting is hard. Then ask why they think it might be important to learn to wait.
- Tell over stories from your own life about how working for or waiting for something actually made you appreciate it more once you got it.

📖 Teachable Moment

- Mastering waiting for a turn is a strong exercise to develop your children's patience muscles. The only way to get better at waiting to take a turn is to practice. If your child struggles with waiting his turn for the swings or having a turn with his or her favorite toy in the shul groups, don't avoid the park or shul playroom—hold their hand or have them on your lap to stroke their hair while they wait. This reinforces the need to be courteous and patient, all the while showing them you are there for them as calming input during the waiting. The repetition will help them learn to cope with waiting.
- For older children, one area where society has become increasingly impatient is with purchasing habits. Even if you can afford to pay for anything they might need, consider giving them an allowance or encouraging after-school jobs so they can pay for certain predetermined items or outings with friends on their own. Let them learn to be patient while earning the money toward those things.

Tools

- **Timers**: Minutes are meaningless to young children, made more meaningless by the fact that we say, "in a minute." "One minute" has come to mean, "When I'm ready I'll help you," but since we often don't follow through in those sixty seconds, it makes time even more confusing to them. Use timers to bridge this gap. The next time your child asks for something when you are busy, try saying, "I'm setting the timer for five/ten/fifteen minutes to finish up what I'm doing, and then I'll be ready to help you, play with you, or whatever else you need." The trick though is to actually follow through and be available when the timer goes off. Either they will have solved the problem independently before you get there, or they'll learn that they are capable of waiting for a few minutes. Sand timers or bubble timers are even better because children can actually physically see the passage of time through the visual of the sand/bubbles tumbling to the bottom.
- Choose some projects or family activities that require time and patience, such as planting, sticker mosaics, and slower-moving games like Ticket to Ride, Monopoly, or for younger children, Candy Land. If you choose planting, try to pick something that will almost certainly sprout and remain hearty—like a bean plant—and remind your children to water it and check on its progress daily. They have to show great patience to work with those seeds!

Reinforcement

- Make some "medallions of patience" that your children get to wear after successfully being patient during a long wait, such as on an airplane, at the doctor office, in line with you at a store, or (groan!) a government office.

CHAPTER 9

Circuit 4:
From Attitude to Gratitude

"A person should always accustom himself to say: All that God does is for the good."

Talmud, Berachos 60b

"It's not happiness that brings us gratitude, its gratitude that brings us happiness."

Origin unknown

Several years ago, I received a proud phone call from my son's first-grade teacher. The class was given an assignment to write a letter to someone they wanted to thank, and my son had chosen his school bus driver. In his letter, he thanked the driver for taking him home every day and driving carefully to keep him safe.

The teacher was so impressed by the unique choice of recipient and carefully thought-out gratitude that she took my son to the bus to deliver the letter, even though this hadn't been part of the assignment. It was a very moving experience for both my son and the driver, an aging man who was rarely given attention by the children. He felt recognized and my son felt important for doing the recognizing. Both walked away, or more accurately drove away, happy.

The incident couldn't have come at a more opportune juncture. My son had just reached the age where certain toys and items began being singled out as "cool," and he wanted more and more of them to bring to school. On top of this, he started to develop a mild case of entitlement, where he was confusing wanting things with needing things, and by extension felt he had an inalienable right to receive them.

The letter assignment provided an opportunity for reflection and appreciation that was the perfect segue to beginning a project of gratitude in our home that carefully navigated us away from drowning under the choppy waters of "the gimmes."

The question becomes: how are we to protect our children from the glass-half empty versus glass-half-full syndrome? How can we make them happy for their desires that have been fulfilled versus miserable over their desires that have not?

I believe the secret is to cultivate an environment of gratitude at home. We can help our children learn not only to be happy with what they already have, but also to tune in to all the wonderful mundane gifts of life they have become habituated to and are now taking for granted. Lucky for us as Jews, gratitude is in our spiritual genes.

When she named her fourth son Yehudah (which is a term of recognition and gratitude), our foremother Leah was the first person on record in world history to express gratitude to Hashem. Rabbi Tzadok HaKohen Rabinowitz explains that knowing there were four wives of Yaakov and twelve foretold tribes, Leah had assumed that each wife would be given three sons. When her fourth one came, she recognized that she had been given more than her fair share and expressed this gratitude by way of name choice. From this name came the term for our very nation (*Yehudim*, Jews), expressing a crucial component of our essence.

Other examples abound: We have role models like Dovid HaMelech, who expressed his thanks to God continuously throughout *Sefer Tehillim*, despite (or often within the very moments of) terrible hardships and dangers, and one of the three main components of our daily *Shemoneh Esreh* prayers is expressing gratitude.

How do we unleash these latent strengths in the next generation? How do we cultivate this desired environment and teach our children to be happy with—and appreciate—what they already have? A good first step is initiating daily gratitude journal projects in our homes.

Each child should have their own diary and be encouraged to list (or for younger children the parents can transcribe) just a few things that they are thankful for. It can be as specific to that day as "I aced my test," and "my friend shared his favorite toy," or as general as "God gave me a great family and a body that works."

As children get older and the project progresses, encourage deeper reflections such as "I noticed this friend really went out of her way to include me," or "I noticed Hashem has made me really talented in art." Once they have gotten used to this reflection, it's also good to add the question, "What have I done for others today?"

When compiled daily, the results are palpable. It is incredible to see the bounty of goodness that may otherwise have been forgotten. To use some examples from my own family, there was the sixty-three dollars in "saved-up-for-a-target-item" cash we were able to recoup after my son dropped it in a Target grocery aisle and a good Samaritan chose to turn it in to the security desk rather than pocket it. There was the time a car almost hit my daughter, who had run into the street, but the driver slammed on his brakes just in time. There was the time I went into labor while my husband was out of town and he managed to tear through the airport, slide through airport security, and hop on a flight that got him to me in time for the birth. This exercise certainly gives new meaning to the verse, "I will give thanks to God with my whole heart; I will recount all of Your wonderful deeds."[1]

At the end of the year, right before Rosh Hashanah, it is an incredibly powerful experience to hand each child their journal and have them review all the goodness that was done for them both by God and man, and that which they have done for others as well. It also serves as a sharp tool to help pull a child out of the doldrums and give them perspective when they are going through a rough patch, since (as we noted in circuit 1) children are prone to all-or-nothing thinking, and when

---

1   *Tehillim* 9:1.

they have a bad day, they sometimes suddenly think their whole life is bad. By showing them their hand-crafted compilation representing all kinds of good things in their lives, it helps them remember how great their lives really are.

A next step is to periodically incorporate larger projects such as writing letters of gratitude. Whether it is to a parent, teacher, or friend (or bus driver for that matter), it's a meaningful exercise to have our children write a letter specifying just how much someone's actions meant to them. At follow-up assessments, studies have shown that people who write these letters report being happier one week—and even one month—later.[2]

Other studies on gratitude show that participants who were given opportunities to practice gratitude felt better about what they had in their life as a whole, were twenty-five percent happier, kept better care of their health, and were more optimistic about the future than study participants who had not been instructed to practice gratitude. Don't write those thank-you cards for your children after they are given gifts—make them do it!

Along with these projects comes developing a culture of gratitude in our homes in general. Being part of a family means helping out, but it does our children a disservice if we show them that everyday activities that are done for them or by them are not worthy of a thank you. When we thank our children for their help, they are likely to start noticing more of the countless everyday things we do for them (and will hopefully generate one or two thank-yous as well).

Make sure the children see you and your spouse thanking each other, and you thanking others out there in the world as well. Be it be a busboy at a restaurant or the worker in the store who showed you the right aisle, thankfulness begets thankfulness and soon the whole family will feel better about what they have.

---

2   Amit Kumar and Nicholas Epley, "Undervaluing Gratitude: Expressers Misunderstand the Consequences of Showing Appreciation," *Psychological Science*, 2018.

We instruct our children from a young age to start their day with *Modeh Ani*. With a little work, they can end their day in *Modeh Ani* mode as well.

Where to Begin: Takeaways and Tips

🗩 Discussion Starters

- Try to ask your children at the dinner table each night to list something they are grateful for.
- Ask your older children if there is anything they learned from their experiences that day.

➔ Ready for Action

- Thank your children when they help you.
- Go out of your way to thank others in front of your children so they see you modeling gratitude.
- Find exercises to grow your own gratitude as well. My husband and I created a WhatsApp group between us that is like a marriage gratitude log. In it, we thank each other for things the other person did. Getting a surprise thank-you message in the middle of the day goes a long way.

🛠 Tools

- Start a gratitude journal for each child.
- Do a letter-writing project where you have your children write thank-you letters to those to whom they feel gratitude.
- Ask your children to write their own thank-you notes when they get gifts. It can be tedious but is an important exercise in planting gratitude.

📊 Reinforcement

- Praise your children when you see them expressing gratitude on their own.

CHAPTER 10

Circuit 5:
Grit

"לְפוּם צַעֲרָא אַגְרָא—*According to the effort is the reward.*"

Pirkei Avos 5:26

"Grit is living life like it's a marathon, not a sprint."

Angela Duckworth

During my childhood, I was a dabbler. I took a session here or there of everything from gymnastics and ice-skating to charcoal drawing and sewing. I tooted a flute for about a year, and my longest extracurricular stint was probably at the piano where I (not-so-adeptly) banged on the keys for approximately seven years (but mostly enjoyed my teacher's frozen oatmeal cookies during song breaks). I got really into basketball for a year and I went to the park every day before the girls' team tryouts to practice my free throws (swishing every single one at the tryouts and being appointed team captain), but then once again moved myself to the sidelines after a year. In short, if there had been an Olympic sport in playing a few musical notes while drawing some crude charcoal drawings on ice-skates, I could have been a contender. I didn't stick to anything long enough to take it to the next level (except perhaps frozen-oatmeal-cookie eating).

The one thing that sticks out in my mind as something I gave my all to without giving up was learning to ride a bike. I have a brother two years older than me and the childhood competition between us was fierce. He learned to ride a bike with ease around age eight, and as I watched him zip around our cul-de-sac, I couldn't help but want to fly too. For days and days I cajoled my father to take me to the parking lot down the street (the same place as the infamous practice during my "basketball dabbling"), and together we spent hours practicing with him holding my bike seat, running behind me and trying to let go without me flying off or falling over. Only problem was that I was not very talented on two wheels. Finally, my father gently told me that perhaps I was too young and we should wait until I was older, but I would have none of it. I decided to continue alone and teach myself. I worked at it again and again, bruising my elbows and cutting my knees, until finally one day I was zipping around the cul-de-sac too, giving my brother a run for his money and my surprised parents a big smile. I had done it—I had stuck with it, put my all into it, and (finally) seen results. And thus, after this, the simple and free activity of riding a bike stands out in my memory as my favorite childhood extracurricular activity, over all of those expensive options that my parents ultimately let me quit.

The secret sauce here was grit, or in other words, following through on what was started. This involves sticking with something even though it is hard for us, or when we don't yet see its value or benefits. It is a quality that seems to be becoming scarcer, and yet it is an important component of success.

Grit and reaching for lofty goals—even when they require dusting ourselves off and trying something hard again and again—is part of our Jewish heritage. In *Mishlei* (24:16), we are told "כִּי שֶׁבַע יִפּוֹל צַדִּיק וָקָם—A righteous person falls seven times and gets up." There are many homiletic interpretations of this. Some say that it is the nature of how he falls that leads to the rising, some say it's the fact that he is able to pick himself back up so many times that makes him into a *tzaddik*. But the crucial factor in this is that someone who becomes a *tzaddik* knows that you can't stop working; you have to keep getting back up until you are the person you are meant to be.

The *Rambam* says in *Hilchos Teshuvah* (5:2) that anyone can become a righteous person like Moshe Rabbeinu or an evil person like Yeravam ben Navat. It's all about putting in the work in the right department. There is a great story about the Alter of Kelm who was trying to keep difficult hours of learning and was missing much sleep as a result. His *talmidim* said, "Rebbe, you are not the Vilna Gaon" (who was known for learning almost twenty-four hours a day and barely getting any sleep). He responded very astutely, "If I hadn't tried to be like the Vilna Gaon, I would have never become the Alter of Kelm." Pushing ourselves to excel and having grit is in our blood; it's just that we need to find the right way to awaken that power in each individual.

The question that comes up for parents is what exactly is the right recipe to engender this important virtue? First off, following through with extracurricular activities has been shown to engender grit. Extracurriculars need to be done for more than a year to have these results. Dr. Margo Gardner[1] did a study following eleven thousand American teens until they were twenty-six years old to see what effect high-school participation in extracurriculars for one year versus two or more had on success rates. Gardner found that children who participated for one year or more were more likely to graduate from college and to volunteer in their community, and those who stuck with it further, for two years or more, were also more likely to be employed as a young adult and have higher incomes.

Angela Duckworth, author of the book *Grit* and beloved professor during my years at the University of Pennsylvania, also found that following through on our commitments both requires grit *and* builds it. She instituted the "Hard Thing Rule" in her home, wherein every family member had to choose (and commit to doing) one hard thing and not quit until the season or tuition payment or other natural stopping point was up. The key here, though, was that everyone got to pick the commitment themselves and thereby took ownership over it. Also,

---

1   Research scientist at the National Center for Children and Families.

everyone was bolstered in knowing they were challenging themselves in their varied interests together.

Consider instituting this in your home. For parents, this could be a commitment to follow a new interest (learning yoga, committing to extra Torah learning, getting a new licensure within your degree) and for children this could be sports team participation, a learning project, or extracurricular talent. It's about a family commitment to both follow your fascination and to not give up. It builds grit muscle memory and stick-to-itiveness.

Duckworth found in her research that high expectations (demanding parenting), coupled with unflagging support (supportive parenting), was the right grit recipe from the parental end. Teachers can also have a strong influence on grit-building with children. In a study run by researchers David Yaeger and Geoff Cohen, seventh-grade teachers were asked to hand back essays with two different responses, one with a general statement and one with a statement of high expectations plus unflagging support. The ones with high expectations and encouragement generated more essay revision by the students! The placebo group's general response Post-its read: *I'm giving you these comments so that you'll have feedback on your paper* (forty percent of these students revised their essays). The high-expectations-plus-encouragement feedback group got Post-its that read: *I'm giving you these comments because I have very high expectations and I know that you can reach them* (eighty percent of these students revised their essays).[2]

The next piece, according to Duckworth, is modeling a strong work ethic and other "gritty" tendencies yourselves. In a study done by Dr. Benjamin Bloom, almost without exception the supportive and demanding parents were "models of the work ethic in that they were hard workers, they did their best in whatever they tried, they believed that work should come before play, and that one should work toward distant goals."

---

2   David Yeager, Gregory Walton, and Geoffrey L. Cohen, "Addressing achievement gaps with psychological interventions," *Kappan Magazine*, p. 65.

In sum, Duckworth says, "Growing up with support, respect, and high standards offers a lot of benefits, one of which is especially relevant to grit." So don't be afraid to push your children, and even more so, don't be afraid to push yourself. Try something new, talk about your work ethic and how you push through things that are hard for you (and if you don't, now is a good time to start). Take out your bike, dust off your flute, or pick up whatever else you dabbled in but didn't quite stick to previously. And if you need some energy to start, I'm happy to give you a great oatmeal cookie recipe, à la my paragon-of-patience piano teacher. Just remember to freeze it first.

Where to Begin: Takeaways and Tips

💬 Discussion Starters

- Talk to your children about skills that you struggled with but kept working on until you succeeded.
- If your children are trying to give up, ask them why. Keep asking why after all their answers until you get to the real heart of it. For example:
  Child: "I want to quit ice-skating."
  You: "Why?"
  Child: "Because I don't like it anymore."
  You: "Why?"
  Child: "Because it's too hard."
  You: "Why?"
  Child: "Because I feel silly, everyone else is moving up a level except me."
  You: "Why is that a bad thing?"
  Child: "Because I feel like a failure."
  Aha! This is where you would start talking about how everyone has their own timeline of succeeding, and if she keeps at it, she is likely to move up a level also.

➡ **Ready for Action**

- Try starting the "Hard Thing Rule" in your home.
- Try not to let your children quit at something they started before they see it through.

⚒ **Tools**

- There are many online growth mindset print-ables that you can place around your house as mindset reminders.

▚ **Reinforcement**

Use growth mindset statements and encourage affirmations such as:

- "I can do hard things."
- "This might take time and effort and that's OK."
- "I stick with things and don't give up easily."
- "I am striving for progress, not perfection."
- "I am brave enough to try."
- "I embrace new challenges."

Praise should be specific and sincere. To instill grit, it is important to praise the process and not the person or outcome. For example, praise effort, strategies, and problem-solving skills.

CHAPTER 11

Circuit 6:
Emotional Agility

"Be flexible like a reed and not stiff like a cedar tree."

Talmud, Taanis 20a

"What the caterpillar calls the end of the world, we call a butterfly."

Eckhart Tolle

You can't predict what will happen in your children's lives, and that is one of the scariest realities as we let them go out into the world and spread their wings. After all, while we do everything we can within our own four walls to try to protect them from any harm, there is absolutely no telling what will happen the minute they step out the door. *Literally.*

I once was at a Shabbos meal where the host family had all elementary and high school–age kids; the house was no longer set up safely for free-range toddlers. I spent the lion's share of the meal in "mommy-cam mode," guarding my little guy and watching his every move like a security camera to make sure he didn't get into trouble. As if this wasn't enough of a challenge, I simultaneously attempted scintillating conversation and catching my other kid's grape juice cups mid-spill, all between hurried bites of schnitzel and Nish-Nosh salad. I tried as seamlessly as I could. Proud of my multitasking abilities to concurrently keep both my son and social life alive, we finally got ready to leave. As we herded our family outside, I turned to give a hug to our hostess and say a quick goodbye. In that split-second my toddler fell down their concrete stairs and ended up with an eye so swollen shut he could barely see out of it the next morning.

The guilt laid itself on thick. I was thrown back into the pain of several years earlier when another baby of mine had fallen and broken her leg while I was "on guard" as well. At the hospital that time, I kept pointing to my little daughter and asking the doctors, "Is there something you can give her for her pain?" (At which point, my husband without skipping a beat, could sense my emotional suffering and would point to me instead and ask the same doctor, "Is there something you could give *her* for the pain?") In both situations, I remember berating myself: *Why did I let my guard down? Why did I not keep up my vigilant guard-dog watch to the end?*

The answer is: We are not God! We simply cannot be watching our children every second, and even more so, it is impossible to keep them away from all harm. This is especially true as they get older and the threat is much more subtle and able to slip under our radar than a dramatic tumble-down-a-stairway. There is everything from isolation in camp and being bullied in school, to struggling to keep up academically but being embarrassed to ask for help, or wrestling their own personal demons of self-consciousness or body image issues (to name only a few). So, the best shield we can give them is actually not a crash helmet and padded body suit, but the emotional equivalent, which is what I like to call emotional shock absorbers. Just like on a car, the shock absorbers allow the vehicle to smoothly sail over bumps or go in and out of potholes while the frame adapts to the uneven terrain, the best skill we can give our children is to help them learn to cope in a flexible way when life sails them into rough patches. The concept has other names too, like bestselling author Susan David's term "emotional agility," which really serves as an inoculation against the unknown. It is the power, strength, *emunah* (faith), and confidence to deal with situations that don't go our way. This is a bit different than circuit 12, "Inoculation of Failure," that we will get to later, although it is related.

MINDSET MALFUNCTION

Here we are talking about taking it a step further. Instead of just recognizing the benefits of letting kids work things out for themselves without swooping in to make sure they never fail, here we are talking about teaching a skill to take them to the next level of coping.

Ms. David writes in her book on the topic: "Ask anyone who has achieved his or her biggest goals or whose relationships thrive, and you'll hear the stories of many unexpected detours along the way. What appears to separate those who master these challenges and the ones who get derailed? The answer is agility—emotional agility." She goes on to say that "[e]motionally agile people are not immune to stresses and setbacks. The key difference is that they know how to adapt, aligning their actions with their values and making small but powerful changes that lead to a lifetime of growth."

The first step to helping our children build up these agile shock absorbers is to teach them acceptance. Acceptance of situations helps us stop struggling with our emotions surrounding "shoulds" (*this should not be this way, they shouldn't have acted this way, I shouldn't have to do this*, etc.). Once we are able to secede in our internal battle over "the principle of the matter," we can make better decisions. In the words of *Pirkei Avos* (2:4): "עֲשֵׂה רְצוֹנוֹ כִּרְצוֹנֶךָ"—Make His will your will." If God wanted things to turn out a certain way, try to accept that there is a reason.

Acceptance also helps us "develop confidence in our resilience" says Nataly Kogan, author of *Happier Now* and creator of The Happier Method™. Kogan calls this quite aptly "your emotional immune system." Ms. David takes this further in *Emotional Agility* by teaching other steps as well to achieve this. I will adapt these here.

The first step is to accept thoughts and emotions instead of struggling against them. Have your child take deep breaths if this helps calm their racing mind.

Second, instead of jumping to conclusions, exercise curiosity about experiences. The essential goal here is to navigate the world as it is, not how we want it to be. Make sure you stay in reality or help your children stay in reality, and not let the mind jump to all the possibilities of the "shoulds" and "what ifs" and "how did this happen?" It is as it is now, and it is a critical step to accept that without jumping into action to make the uncomfortable feelings temporarily go away.

Let's turn this into an example. Let's say your child comes home and says, "Some kids in my class spread a rumor about me and now no one will play with me." Don't just say, "You don't need them, I'll play with you!" or "I'll call your teacher and make sure they get in big trouble for what they did." While responding in these ways may solve the problem temporarily, it deprives the child of the critically important opportunity to sit with difficult feelings.

The next step in emotional agility is to teach our children that they are not passive observers in their own lives; they are in the driver's seat and have the ability to choose how they respond in any given situation. We then need to remind our children that how we deal with our inner world drives everything. We don't have control over what happened, but we do have control over our reaction. Ms. David says it best when she writes, "Emotions pass. They are transient. There is nothing in mental experience that *demands* an action." To quote the profound encapsulation of this concept by Viktor Frankl after he survived the ravages of the Holocaust: "Between stimulus and response there is a space. In that space is our power to choose our response. In our response lies our growth and our freedom."[1]

There are several points of vulnerability in any given situation. We have no power over the stimuli in our lives, and yet we have every bit of power over our response. After that response though, we also have no power over the outcome. The *Shaar Bitachon*, in *Chovos Halevavos/ Duties of the Heart* by Rabeinu Bachya Ibn Paquda, says that every human action has three components: The first is the decision to do, the second is our efforts, and the third is the results. The first and second are up to us but the third is up to God. That is where the famous saying, "Let go and let God" comes in strongly again.

One technique for coping is to learn to label our thoughts and emotions as we are having them as just that: thoughts and emotions. This

---

1   From his book, *Man's Search for Meaning* (1946).

distancing creates space between us and what's passing through our heads. "I am feeling stupid, but that is just a thought. It doesn't mean that's the reality of who I am." Learning that we are not everything we think and feel, is one of the most powerful lessons to fight our internal chaos. And when you accomplish this, you can figure out how to unhook and keep going with whatever your task might be, despite fear, hurt, or general distress.

The same two people can experience the same situation and respond totally differently. Two summers ago, I dropped my eldest child off at sleepaway camp for the first time and witnessed so many different responses. There were children running off to talk to their friends, and ones clinging to their parents. There were also parents running off to talk to their friends, and parents clinging to their children! There are so many ways to respond to separation, and yet there is an aspect of choice in the matter. Personally, inside I wanted to be one of those parents clinging to their children, but on the outside I made myself walk off and postpone my emotional upheaval until later that night, for fear I would make it difficult for my son (who was otherwise one of the children separating easily). Stimulus-response: same stimulus, but opposite response. The choice is ours, when we are able to step back and make the space, find that freedom and freeze-frame in between our stimuli and our response.

Another step that Ms. David recommends is connecting with our "why." "Why are you here at camp?" or "Why did you choose to be a mother even though you knew there would be times of distress?" Reminding ourselves of bigger goals makes our shock absorbers more effective as we bump along life's road. Speak to your children about the difference between acting on impulse and acting on your values. What we feel like doing in the moment is sometimes not in alignment with our larger goals. Try to respond to your thoughts and feelings in a way that aligns with who you really want to be and what you really want to do.

Choice is our biggest empowerment as a human being. The *Meshech Chochmah* (*Bereishis* 1:26) says that our *bechirah chofshis* (free choice) is what makes us human because that is the essence of our *tzelem Elokim*, our Godly image. How we navigate the world *as it is* and not on the fantasy of *how we think it should be* is what makes us emotionally agile.

Ultimately, in the words of Susan David, "Rigidity in the face of complexity is toxic." How we deal with our inner world drives everything. Through practice we can learn to be emotionally nimble, and that is what will ultimately set us free from some of the deepest pain in life, the kind that is way worse than a tumble down stairs, a broken leg, or—even worse—the emotional pain that a mother feels when her child is out of her grasp and gets hurt. At the end of the day, despite my husband's question at the hospital really being in jest, there is an accurate answer for "What can you give *her* for the pain?" That answer is emotional agility.

Where to Begin: Takeaways and Tips

💬 Discussion Starters

- Try to explain to your children that we are not everything we think and feel.
- Discuss the Mishnah, "עֲשֵׂה רְצוֹנוֹ כִּרְצוֹנֶךָ—Make His will your will." If God wanted things to turn out a certain way, try to accept that there is a reason.
- Talk to them about how we can't control anything in the world except our own responses.
- Talk to older children about acting on their values instead of their impulses.

➡️ Ready for Action

- Give children plenty of time and space to feel their feelings. Just telling them, "You're OK," or "It was no big deal, get over it," can invalidate their feelings and make them angrier and less emotionally agile. If they have space to fully feel their feelings without our value judgements, those feelings will go away, and they will be ready to move on. For example, think of a kid who gets hit by another kid in the playground. If you tell them, "You're OK, it was barely a tap," they are more likely to make it into a tear-filled drama or sulk on a bench. Contrast this with a kid who runs to their parent for comfort, gets that desired comfort or space to be upset, and then quickly thereafter runs back to the playground as if nothing happened.

- Remind your children that emotions pass and usually there is nothing about being upset that *demands* an action that second. You can always respond to something later, but it is much more difficult to take something back that was said or done rashly.
- Take off your "rescuer cape" ("Don't worry, I'll play with you if no one else wants to!"). Instead, try to help your children accept the current reality ("It sounds like there are some tough personalities in your class. Give it time and it's likely they will warm up to you.").

📖 Teachable Moment

- If your children get mad at themselves for feeling certain emotions (like sadness or anger) after a setback or hurt, try to help them figure out why they feel that way. Help them welcome that feeling, knowing that it has a purpose. Often, when we allow a feeling instead of rejecting it, it feels acknowledged and dissipates.
- Help your child connect with their bigger-picture "why" when they have a setback.

⬚ Reinforcement

- Some people find it helpful to have a statement they say when they are working on accepting something. A famous one is the following: "God, grant me the serenity to accept the things I cannot change, courage to change the things I can, and wisdom to know the difference."[2]

---

2   Reinhold Niebuhr.

CHAPTER 12

Circuit 7:
Mindset Matters—
Frames Form Our Future

"If a person says I have worked hard but have not found [success], don't believe him. [If a person says] I have not exerted myself, and I have found [success], don't believe him. [If he says] I gave it my all and I have found [success], believe him."

Talmud, Megillah 6b

"Never solve a problem from its original perspective."

Charles Thompson

Our mindsets are the glasses of our reality; they distort or enhance everything, each person with their own self-written prescription. In many ways, mindsets reflect our "habits" at looking at things.

Our thoughts are the stories we tell ourselves, which ultimately become our textbook on the world. The only thing is, we are not passive readers or observers of these stories. Ultimately, we are the authors, and that is where mindset and—to break it down a bit further—the frames we use to perceive and interpret the world, become our ink.

In the words of Adam Sicinski, founder of IQ Matrix and expert on mind mapping, "Framing is a mental structure that is built upon the beliefs you have about yourself, your roles, your circumstances, and about other people. It is a structure you use to ascribe meaning to given circumstances. In other words, the meaning you ascribe to any event is dependent upon how you frame it in your mind. As such, your frames shape how you see the world, how you see yourself, how you view others, and how you interpret your life."[1]

Try to reflect on some of your own mental biases:

- Do you see the world within the frame of everyone either hating you or liking you? For example, if you don't receive an expected invitation in the mail to a *simchah*, do you assume the *baal simchah* purposely left you out, or do you think it was potentially lost in the mail or an accidental oversight?

- Do you look through a frame that assumes people are good and trying to help you or that they are bad and trying to cheat you? For example, if your bill at a check-out was rung up incorrectly, would you think it was a purposeful plot to overcharge you or would you think it was simply an honest mistake?

When several people come upon an interaction or similar circumstance, they can each leave with a completely different interpretation, depending on their mental frames. As an example, let's say there are three people who encounter the same friend in different aisles of a grocery store. Since this friend is late for an appointment, she brushes them off when they try to engage her in conversation in an effort to quickly grab her final shopping items and hurry out of the store.

- Person One sees the world through the "no one likes me" frame. She internalizes judgments and takes the grocery store interaction personally. She sees the friend's behavior as a snub and she feels bad about herself because this is just another example of how no one wants to talk to her.

---

1   https://blog.iqmatrix.com/reframing-thoughts.

- Person Two sees the world through the "people are bad" frame. She externalizes judgements and sees the friend's behavior in the grocery store as rude, chalking it up to another example of people selfishly just doing whatever is convenient for them, even if it means hurting a friend.

- Person Three feels pretty good about the world. She generally experiences situations through a frame of "when people act out of the ordinary there must be a reasonable explanation." With this frame, she correctly is able to assess that the grocery store situation has nothing to do with her personally, and it is also not a reflection of who the rushed friend is at her core. Rather, she assumes this friend has something going on that caused her to act in an uncharacteristically aloof manner.

It is in this way that frames are linked to an underlying belief and/ or assumption that is implied by our thoughts, and they will color our entire reading of interactions and events. Obviously, the third frame is the most helpful one to try to develop because often, when people act in an unusual way (yell at us, snub us, etc.), it has absolutely nothing to do with us and everything to do with them. In an interaction, we only see part of the story and have no idea what happened in the person's day beforehand, nor do we know what they are dreading later on in their day.

We have automatic frames and intentional ones. When we are self-reflective enough to tease these apart, we can identify which ones we choose more intentionally. We can then try to improve these as an easy first step.

Children are not mature enough to be this self-reflective, so we can do some of this work for them. Like the process we talked about with Pilot Light Motivations, it is helpful to start viewing our children with the thought of "What frames are they using to interpret the world?"

Mindset and frames are important to work on with children for many reasons. We use frames to solve problems, get a better understanding of the long-term consequences of decisions and actions, connect unrelated events and circumstances, and to just make more sense of the world in general. Since a large part of childhood involves making sense of an unfamiliar world, positive frames are even more important for children. They will help create their baseline understanding of the world, and this will follow them through the rest of their lives. Frames allow us to gather unique understandings of our experiences and thus affect how we act moving forward.

Frames also help us handle feedback and criticism. For example, consider a scenario in which a child gets a bad grade on an essay. If they view themselves through an "I'm stupid" frame, the bad grade will be perceived as futher proof of that self-deprecating assumption. In contrast, a child with an "I'm smart" frame might say, "I know I could have done better. I wonder what I could improve on for next time?"

Another common mindset in children is the "all-or-nothing" mindset, related to the all-or-nothing thinking that we spoke about in circuit 1. Children are prone to seeing things in black and white, which makes them feel like current situations are unchangeable. For example, after falling down a few times during a first ice-skate/bike/walk the balance beam lesson, a child's all-or-nothing frame might make them say, "I'll never be able to do it." Or, after not being invited to a classmate's birthday party, this frame might make them interpret it as, "nobody likes me." And after fighting over a toy with a sibling, this frame might make them go to an extreme: "My sister is always mean to me. I hate her!"

The best antidote to this kind of mindset malfunction is to get children to keep trying despite these thoughts, and after they inevitably succeed, to point out how their initial catastrophic failure predictions or always-horrible relationship predictions were actually incorrect.

When it comes to misfortunes, they are rarely as bad as the brain registers them. And yet, we intensely register them, both in childhood and adulthood. So much so, in fact, that the mind hardly ever "dwells" on the positive.

Scientists say that we are hardwired with what they have dubbed the "negativity bias." This bias makes the brain like a magnet for negative experiences and a nonstick cooking pan for positive ones, but it actually exists for our own survival. To keep us out of harm's way, negative events grab our mind's attention more than positive ones. Think about how many times your brain replays a good experience versus a negative one, how much your mind wanders to a positive situation instead of a negative one, or a past success rather than a failure. Do we think about all the parts of our body that are feeling normal and great, or about that one thing in our health that is not where we want it to be? Do we think about all the good interactions we had over the course of a day or do we single out the one that made us feel bad?

MINDSET
MALFUNCTION

We tend to overestimate threats and underestimate possibilities. Without realizing it, we cloud our glasses with the wrong prescription: the negativity lens. We then look at the world and see the same monotonous job, the same inconsiderate family members, and the daily aches and pains.

Experts tell us that it takes three positive thoughts to offset one negative thought. So how do we actively work on reframing?

When children are complaining about a situation and it is clear they are using their negativity bias or "nobody likes me" frame, try to help them ask:

- "Could it be there was a positive intention here?"
- "What would I prefer their actions or words to really mean?"
- "Does this really have to do with me, or is this about the other person?"

I have found this third question to be the most helpful reframe when trying to make sense of disappointing interpersonal interactions. We are all naturally self-centered because we spend all our time with ourselves and view everything through our own eyes. Therefore, from a primal standpoint, we interpret everything as having to do with us as an *automatic* response. However, when we are able to use the "Does this really have to do with me?" reframe as part of our *intentional* response, we can get to a more realistic picture on what occurred. This strategy is called broadening our scope.

Another strategy is to focus on the upside of a downside situation. Many losses contain a gain if you look for it. Ask, "Is there anything positive you can find in this?" If your child says no, try another strategy, this time looking for an opportunity for growth. Think of a setback as a lesson to grow from instead of a failure to endure. Ask what they can learn from difficult outcomes or failures in order to use them as stepping stones.

Lastly, we can pinpoint the opportunity contained in the difficulty. Ask, "How can you make this situation work to your advantage?" Sometimes a closing door leads to more opportunities. I would be remiss here if I didn't quote my beloved grandmother's oft-said phrase, "One bus goes, another one comes." This was an incredible reframe, coming from a Holocaust survivor who lost so much of her family before immigrating to a new country and struggling financially most of her life. She was always looking for the new opportunity when the old one ended; she was full of grit and a perspective of purpose. Her daughter, my Aunt Mindy, internalized this lesson from her mother as well, recognizing that when one opportunity ended, there was no reason to doubt that new help or an opportunity wasn't already on the way. On several occasions, as *chizuk* to not fall into despair, I heard her quote the famous line from *Megillas Esther* (4:14), "רֶוַח וְהַצָּלָה יַעֲמוֹד לַיְּהוּדִים מִמָּקוֹם אַחֵר—Relief and help will come up for the Jews from another place!"

The last strategy is to help our children notice the words they use when they are speaking: "Are you using positive or negative language?" Negative language activates our negativity bias. Positive language, even when faked, can lift our emotions—just like smiling even when we don't feel like it has been shown to improve people's moods. Recent studies indicate that repeated smiling rewires your brain to create more positive patterns.[2]

So smile, and write yourself a new prescription for mindset frames, one that reflects the intentions of how you want to see the world, to replace your automatic processing that has degraded and clouded your vista over time. Put those new ones over your eyes, and order matching ones for your family. The world will look much brighter when you do.

---

2 Paul Ekman and Richard J. Davidson, "Voluntary Smiling Changes Regional Brain Activity," *Psychological Science* 4, 5 (1993): 342–45.

Where to Begin: Takeaways and Tips

💬 Discussion Starters

- Talk to your children about the negativity bias.
- Ask in a down situation whether there is any upside or opportunity your children can see within the difficulty?
- When a child is complaining about an interpersonal situation and it is clear they are using their negativity bias or "nobody likes me" frame, try to help them ask:
  - "Could it be there was a positive intention here?"
  - "What would I like what they did or said to really mean?"
  - "Does this really have to do with me? Or is this about the other person?"

➡️ Ready for Action

- Work on adjusting mindset malfunctions: Get children to keep trying despite self-deprecating thoughts, and after they inevitably succeed, point out how their initial catastrophic failure predictions or always-horrible relationship predictions were actually incorrect.
- Try to figure out the frames your children are using to make sense of the world (such as in the example in the chapter).

CHAPTER 13

Circuit 8: Teaching a Timeline Perspective

"A person should be willing to give up all his tomorrows for one today, so that he doesn't end up wasting all his todays on one tomorrow."

The Alter of Novardok

"Time not only heals, time reveals."

Karen Salmansohn

As I have gotten older, time has spun off course. The months of June through August used to pass at a languidly paced, delightfully tiptoeing summer rhythm, but now seem to race by in the blink of an eye. Likely you have felt it too—that pull of the clock, speeding through your weeks, fast-forwarding your life year by year so that each twelve-month calendar seems tossed in the recycle bin faster than the last. Why is this? Quite simply, it's just that the more time has passed under our belts, the more we have behind us to compare it to. In other words, to a ten-year-old, their first decade seems like it took forever because quite literally, so far it *has been* their forever. But for a fifty-year-old who has gone through the decade-long cycle five times, ten years doesn't seem like forever because it was only a fifth of their life thus far.

Our children's resulting challenge is that it is very hard for them to have a timeline perspective. Children live "in the moment" much more than we do (for better or worse), so if they feel bad about something right now, it is hard for them to look ahead and fathom that they won't feel bad about it later.

This is especially challenging for teenagers—and even young adults. It's the unspoken (or sometimes, unfortunately, spoken) attitude of "If I don't go to this party, the world is going to end"; "If you don't get me the new shoes that all of my friends are wearing, the world is going to end"; "If I don't get into this particular seminary, my whole life's path will be thrown off course, and (yes you guessed it,) the world is going to end."

We know from our own lives that this is usually not true. How many times did we plan for things that turned out a different way, but we later realized was for the best? And even the times it didn't feel best for us, we were still able to recognize that the world nonetheless went on spinning. We can look back and understand or accept why things happened a certain way, but this benefit of perspective literally only happens with the passage of enough time (which children just don't have). Hindsight is 20/20, but only for those who can turn around, adjust their glasses, and see a vista.

Working on teaching our children a timeline perspective is a helpful tool. Try to gently speak to them about this by asking whether something that is upsetting them will still be bothering them tomorrow. If they say yes, continue by asking about next week, next month, next year. The key to the exercise is noticing that feelings and situations don't last forever. Try to help children notice the transient nature of their emotions. If they still dig in and say, "I'll be upset about this forever," then catch them the next day, or week, or when *you* see they have calmed down and ask whether they are still upset about that thing you questioned them about earlier. Even if they refuse to admit that we were right, it's likely they will take note internally that, "Hmmm, I guess that wasn't as big a deal as I made it out to be."

The power of systematically realizing that eventually you won't be thinking about your current problem, slight, or social implosion, helps you remember that problems are transient, and life is much bigger than this moment. A friend of mine who is a psychologist mentioned to me that even thoughts of harming oneself often revolve around not being able to see into the future and realize that things can get better and change with time.

As much as you can, share stories from your own life about situations that bothered you but then dissipated, times when you thought you would never get over something and yet you did. Even if our children don't have enough time in their current journey to totally get this concept, at least they can learn from our lengthier timelines.

I've told my children stories that fit the bill from various eras of my life: About the alleged friend who spread false rumors about me before we started high school, and how I showed up the first day and got a weird vibe from everyone and never wanted to go back. I then tell them how my parents forced me to go back on day two and then three, four, five...three hundred, and how step-by-step, I proved the rumors wrong, made a giant group of friends, many of whom are still among my closest friends to this day. I then tell them how I even later forgave and befriended that girl who spread the rumors, and while I won't tell my children who she is, she has even been to our home.

I tell them about how Abba and I looked to buy a house for over a year, desperate to get out of our living situation: at that time, we had no choice but to sleep with all our children in the shul where my husband was a *rav* every Shabbos because our interim apartment wasn't close enough to walk. I explain how after that year, I finally found a house that met all of our needs and I was so thrilled to sign the contract. I was eight months pregnant and dreamed of bringing the baby home from the hospital to our new home, only to have the contract terminated by the seller on Purim day as I approached my ninth month. I tell my children how I cried and cried, certain that we would never find another house in the area like that one. I then tell them the crescendo of the story: how we gave up and were about to put an offer on a mediocre house just for the sake of moving anywhere, when a well-priced but dilapidated fixer-upper with an amazing lot came on the market and we threw all caution to the wind and made an offer on its first day on the market. We ended up signing the contract the day before I gave birth and while it took a year to get the permits and fix it up, it ended up more beautiful than the first house ever would have ever been, and I thank God for making that previous offer fall through.

At age-appropriate stages, I also tell them the harder stories: the ones where everything did not turn out rosy, where I had to deal with things that didn't go my way even in the long term, and how I got back up and moved on anyway. How eventually a day turned into a week, a month, a year, and before I knew it, somewhere in that whirlwind of time, I was over it and on to bigger and better things—all part of the *berachah* of the healing power of time that God imbued the world with.

All this leads me of course to Hashem, the inroad that all things travel back to. Another amazing tool for successfully instilling a timeline perspective is to help our children tap into the infinite. When we talk to them about God and this amazing world He created that has been around for millennia, and when we discuss our history, traditions, and heritage, it helps our children realize that things are much bigger than they are. Quite literally, everything becomes broader when you have Hashem in your life. We can read stories to our children from books about *emunah* and *hashgachah pratis* (Divine intervention), about situations where there seemed to be no way things could work out for the best, and yet they did. The dinner table and Shabbos table are ideal places to share stories from the day or week in which we personally saw God helping us solve a problem as well. We try to do so quite often in our family from the dining room table, smack in the middle of that fixer-upper, bought-at-the-buzzer house that I'm so glad we had the timeline perspective to wait for.

Where to Begin: Takeaways and Tips

💬 Discussion Starters

- Talk to your children about how feelings change when you give them time, even when you are so upset that you can't imagine feeling better.
- Talk to your older children about times in your life when things didn't work out as you had hoped, but you later realized it was really for the best. Also talk about the times when things still didn't appear for the best, but despite residual pain, you eventually came to a place of acceptance.

➡ Ready for Action

- Read aloud *hashgachah pratis* stories about situations that seemed hopeless until Hashem swooped in to make them work out. (There are many beautiful compilations, such as *Living Emunah* by Rabbi David Ashear.)
- Make a family miracles journal recording times when you felt Divine intervention in your lives.

📖 Teachable Moment

- When your children are upset, use the "Will this still be bothering you in a day, week, month?" exercise. (You can even go up to next year with this inquiry.)
- Remind them that the world is much bigger than this particular moment in time.

Action

CHAPTER 14

Circuit 9:
Identifying Strengths

"A person should always push away with his [weak] left hand, but draw near with his [strong] right hand."

Rus Rabbah 2

"A tool is just an opportunity with a handle."

Kevin Kelly

"This is the time of day where I tell you something great about you." When she was around five years of age, I would say this statement to start a daily conversation with one of my daughters. She happened to be my middle child at the time, and I felt she could really benefit from this routine. Having been a middle child myself, I knew what it was like to feel "passed over," with the parental attention often unintentionally focused on the oldest or youngest child. My daughter was (and is) a fabulous kid, and I wanted her to know that I was noticing her. Moreover, I realized that even more important than *my noticing* her utter fabulousness, was *her* knowing it about herself. Each day, the activity took only a minute or two: some days I'd remind her of a character trait she excelled at, some days I'd tell her something exceptional she had done when she was younger, and some days I pointed out an incident from just a few hours before that really struck me as advanced or caring or creative or whatever other positive characteristic she had exemplified. The results were palpable—I could see her confidence growing and her joy showing.

Self-confidence is a crucial component of happiness at any age, and yet it's becoming a scarcer commodity in our society.[1] This makes it harder and harder to fill our children up with it. I attended a workshop on instilling self-confidence in children, where the lecturer began by showing a picture of an adorable baby in a bucket. The only problem? The bucket was filled with holes and water was pouring out. A quote by Alvin Price elaborates upon this visual message: "Parents need to fill a child's bucket of self-esteem so high that the rest of the world can't poke enough holes to drain it dry." In other words, we as parents need to fill up our children with so much love and confidence that when the rest of the world pokes holes in their feelings of self-worth, our children won't get depleted.

Parents have a unique role in this because from an early age our children are looking for our approval. As they grow older, they might say they "don't care what we think," but this simply isn't true. Suniya Luthar, a famous psychologist and researcher in the area of vulnerability and resilience, says that while she can't list all the components of good parenting, she is reasonably sure about what parents should avoid: "Our research consistently found if there is one thing related to problems of all kinds, it is being highly criticized by your parents," she said. "It is one of the most powerful risk factors."

We need to find a way to guide our children, help them improve on their character traits, and succeed in general without tearing them down. They need us to be the ones telling them "what is great about them" because there is nothing as stabilizing for children as knowing that their parents believe in them and are on their sides. Criticism is necessary, as we are our children's moral compasses and reality shapers for many years of their lives, but excessive criticism becomes toxic.

---

1   https://bit.ly/2GBAkIW.

A key component to developing self-confidence and security is teaching our children to discover, recognize, and embrace their own strengths. Everyone is given their own toolbox of *kochos* (strengths), be it in the realm of academic intelligence, social intelligence, artistic talent, athleticism, or *middos*. By teaching our children to appreciate what's in their own toolbox and embracing the fact that everyone has a different toolbox to work with, they are able to be more confident and home in on what they do best.

The next step is to understand that naturally, along with their personal mix of special strengths, come weaknesses as well. Weaknesses should be looked at carefully, in a way that helps children see the areas they need to work on or accept those in which they may never excel. However, this should always be done inwardly vis-à-vis *themselves*. The work here is for *both* the parents and the children. We have to stop ourselves from comparing our children to others and asking questions such as, "Why can't you be more like your sister?" or "How come you don't work as hard as that child in your class with the great grades?" Asking these questions is missing the point. We can always try to *improve* our children, to take their raw material and sharpen their strengths or dull their weaknesses, but it's an exercise in futility to try to *change* who they are and make them into other people.

The next step after helping our children identify their strengths and weaknesses is to teach them to embrace the fact that each group of abilities was given to them by God as part of a Divine custom-made toolbox. The purpose of these tools is to achieve the successes and confront the challenges they will face in their lives. In other words, we can teach our children that everyone is given a variety of *keilim* (tools) to help them navigate this world, and each toolbox has been tailor-made by the Creator of the Universe to help each individual succeed in their own adventures. In the words of Rabbi Eliyahu Dessler: "It makes as little sense for me to covet [what my neighbor has] as for a watchmaker to covet the tools of a road maker, or for a shortsighted person to covet the spectacles prepared for a farsighted one. Tools are obviously only good for their purpose." Therefore, it is futile to be jealous and wish you had someone else's tools. After all, if you need to fix a problem in your life—why would you look in someone else's toolbox?

It can't be denied that some children are naturally more confident than others. We all know people who seem to have been born feeling comfortable in their own skin, while others never seem to feel quite right, as if they always have on the wrong skin size or style. We can't change our children's confidence overnight, just like we would never think that we can change our own. But we can certainly start with the small steps of identifying their strengths and helping them accept their limitations.

Where to Begin: Takeaways and Tips

💬 Discussion Starters

- List aloud to your children every category of *kochos* you can think of: academic intelligence, social intelligence, artistic talent, athleticism, sense of humor, raw *middos*, and more. Then:
  - Ask your children what they think their strengths are from each category.
  - Add on what you think their strengths are as well.
  - Ask them to share what they think each of their sibling's strengths are. (If they feel hesitant about complimenting their siblings directly, you can try the following game: tape a sheet on each person's back and give everyone a pen to go around the room, writing the strengths they see in each sibling on their backs so no one knows who wrote what.) This helps children see that other people notice their strengths and believe in their abilities!
- Privately ask your children what they think their weaknesses might be and see if you can show them how to use the strengths to overcome these weaknesses.

✕ Tools

- Teach your children to set and achieve goals, and through this they can learn about their strengths/weaknesses.
- Give them tasks around the house that bring out their strengths.

▪▪ Reinforcement

- Try to have a certain time of day or week where you do the "here's when I tell you what's great about you" exercise, reviewing each child's best moments and qualities that shone through during that time period.

CHAPTER 15

Circuit 10:
Harnessing Habits

*"Habits create mastery over matters, and all
beginnings are difficult."*

Igeres HaGra, citing Shaarei Teshuvah and Mechilta

*"The chains of habit are too weak to be felt until
they are too strong to be broken."*

Samuel Johnson

Adults are often heard waxing philosophical about willpower. It's hard to maintain resolve, and for several decades there was science to back slip-ups. In the 1990s, psychologist Roy Baumeister first proposed the image of self-control as a muscle that gets tired over time. For a long while people bought into that. They'd explain away why the willpower they were exerting so much for, let's say, exercising every morning instead of hitting the snooze button, left them with not enough energy remaining for other areas that needed willpower, such as not yelling at their kids. The depletion frame was convenient; it made us feel absolved when we failed, and the only teeny-tiny problem was that it wasn't all that true.

A new generation of psychologists, unable to replicate the studies that initially led to this idea of "ego depletion," have moved on to other models that reveal more of reality. Researchers are finding that "controlling our impulses" or "making good choices" can become more of an automated response through habit, leaving less to the wiles of willpower and more to the superpower of routine.

Whether we realize it or not, a lot of our daily behavior is composed of habits, and so is the behavior of our children. Habits are kind of like our internal programmed settings: automatic behaviors that we do without thinking. If you reflect deeply on this, there are things we do the same way or in the same sequence every day. Think of the way you take a shower, the way you get ready to leave the house, the way you get ready for bed. My husband claims that for a man to describe how he puts on his tefillin is almost impossible; it quickly develops into an intricate process that his brain takes over and files away into the automatic settings.

If you go through the day piece by piece, you will be shocked to know how much of what you do is on the autopilot (or auto-*person*) setting. Think about the last time you roamed the grocery store looking for new products, rather than throwing the same staples in your cart. Think about the last time you ordered something you had never tried from a restaurant. The answer to both is probably "not recently." Habits are everywhere, and best of all, we are often unaware of them.

Rabbi Chaim Friedlander tells the following story of Rabbi Yerucham of Mir. He was once traveling, and he stayed with people who woke in the middle of the night for a meal. When he asked them why they did this, they responded with surprise, questioning how anyone could possibly go through a night *without* waking to eat! This story powerfully shows how habit drives whatever we are used to and can even alter our physiological make up. Imagine a whole group of people who felt hunger pains in the night and had to wake up to eat, just because they trained their bodies over time to have this physiological response!

Before you panic that you have become a robot, know that most habits are truly a good thing. In fact, let us turn to harnessing the power of habits to help our children (and maybe even ourselves) need less willpower.

Habit work can help the impulsive child, the scatterbrained child, the chronically running-late child, the tough-to-put-to-bed child, and a whole other host of categorical childhood characters. Habits allow them (and us) to work actions into our machinery as opposed to relying so heavily on "controlling ourselves" or preplanning.

The first step is to figure out what new habit or habitual routine will help improve the problem area. For example, let's say there is a child who is always leaving their homework at school. You might decide that the habit they need is to put homework directly in their backpack whenever it is given out. Well, that's all well and good but they are probably not allowed to run to their hallway locker whenever they are handed a worksheet. You might therefore decide they need a specific folder for their homework to carry with them all day, with the understanding that you will help them sort it out at home. A good "catch-all" homework folder should be very brightly colored and hard to miss. That way, if all else fails and they leave it in their bag all day, at least it will hopefully catch their attention as they pack up their bag to leave. The sight of it will be a visual cue to scramble, gather, and shove in all their homework.

Another helpful tool is to create routine charts. These can be lifesavers for chronically late children, especially those who are not at the door in time to go to school. It is likely they are having trouble remembering all the steps to getting ready in the morning, and they end up rushing around frantically. A routine chart with the order of every task can make the sequence more into a habit, kind of like the sequencing habits people form for showering (are you a wash-your-hair-first or a wash-your-hair-last type? Notice that you almost never do it in the opposite order, even though you totally could).

Here is an example of a morning routine chart:

- Wash *negel vasser.*
- Use the bathroom and do everything else you need to do in the bathroom while you are already there: brush teeth, comb hair, shower if necessary.
- Go back to your room and get dressed.
- Eat breakfast.
- Put your lunchbox in your bag.
- Pack up homework and other items you want to bring that day to school.
- Put on shoes and coat.

Some children need a nighttime routine chart instead to prevent morning panic. Signs of morning panic that could have been prevented by a better nighttime routine include such statements as: "Oh no, I forgot to do my homework essay! I need fifteen minutes to do it now." "Oh no, I wanted to be the one to bring the football today so I could be quarterback and now I have to spend twenty minutes looking for it all over the overgrown yard!" "Oh no, I can't find any clean uniform skirts and now I have to search through the laundry or change my outfit three times!"

Notice how as a result of each of these scenarios, the entire family is likely to be late.

To prevent these and other delay debacles, a habit-forming nighttime routine chart could look like this:

- Do homework and make sure you put it in your backpack immediately upon completion. Homework that lives on the kitchen table doesn't get turned in and doesn't count!
- Pack backpack with any items you will want to bring to school tomorrow. Think ahead of what you might need so there are no last-minute backpack-loading emergencies.
- Pick out your outfit for tomorrow and place it in a designated spot in your room.
- Turn in any notes from your teachers, tests, or permission slips you need to be signed.
- Mention in advance if you are required to bring in food for a class celebration tomorrow. Don't expect to be able to find twenty-five matching treats in the right quantity last minute before we leave in the morning.
- Please make sure your shoes are by the door ready to be put on in the morning. In winter, pack up your change of shoes and have your boots waiting by the door.

Harnessing habit can also be used for mitzvos! My husband created a "Thirteen Mitzvos Chart" for each of our children to start their days right, and he leaves it at their breakfast spots every morning alongside a coin for *tzedakah*. The sheet includes the six *mitzvos temidios* (constant mitzvos) and six *zechiros* (recollections) so they can read through the list while they wait for breakfast. This way, they start their morning off with thirteen mitzvos (*tzedakah* is #13). Here is the sheet:

Six Mitzvos to Always Remember:

1. Believe in Hashem
2. Believe in One Hashem
3. Love Hashem
4. Fear Hashem
5. Do not believe in other powers
6. Do not be misled by your hearts and your eyes

Six Recollections for Every Day:

1. *Yetzias Mitzrayim*—Hashem taking us out of Egypt
2. *Cheit Ha'egel*—the sin of the Golden Calf
3. *Matan Torah*—the giving and receiving of the Torah
4. *Zecher Miriam*—when Miriam got leprosy for speaking *lashon hara*
5. Shabbos
6. *Zecher Amaleik*—getting rid of the nation of Amalek

The Alter of Kelm also recognized the power of using habit to create mitzvah muscle memory. He told the *bachurim* in his yeshiva to go to the *beis midrash* at times they were not used to going and to learn a five-minute *seder* once there. After five minutes, he instructed them to get up, close the *sefarim* and then leave. He explained that this was to teach their brains that five minutes matters, thus getting them in the habit of taking the time to learn even when they only have a brief window.

The last piece of habit formation is being consistent with the new habit you have chosen to put in place. Habits only form after mentally planting the routine many times. The key is to be patient. According to Benjamin Gardner, lecturer in health psychology, it takes sixty-six days for a habit to become an unconscious part of your routine. To highlight once again the Vilna Gaon's quote at the beginning of this circuit, *"Hergel b'davar shilton*—Habits create mastery over matters...*v'kol haschalos kashos*—although it is hard at the beginning." Don't give up just because the beginning is hard. Stay the course and when habit does strike, the robotic results will be powerful.

Don't leave it up to chance, willpower (or won't-power). Make it a household habit to build habits instead.

Where to Begin: Takeaways and Tips

➡ Ready for Action

- Brainstorm which habits will fix problem areas.
- Make routine charts.
- Make mitzvos habit charts.
- Stick with the new action and be consistent until the habit is formed.

▪ Reinforcement

- Reward new habit success: consider rewarding with experiences and not items.

CHAPTER 16

Circuit 11:
The Power of Reminders

"What the child says out in the street comes either
from his father or his mother."

Talmud, Sukkah 56b

"Keep your 'why' close by."

Weight Watchers

Years ago, I was looking to get off the diet roller coaster. After various pregnancies, I had climbed aboard and buckled myself into low carb, Weight Watchers, and no sugar/no flour, each with its own success—but my cravings for the cocoa bean always lured me back with a clarion call that would push me into freefall. The issue with me (at least I always told myself) was the lack of willpower. I could keep diets up for a couple months but once I had reached a major part of my goal, it was the maintenance phase that eluded me. How was one to keep up willpower for such a long period of time with chocolate lurking around every corner and *kiddush* table? It was then that I came across books by Dr. Judith Beck, a master of cognitive behavior therapy, that connected the methods of CBT to dieting. In other words, it wasn't any particular eating plan that created magic, it was merely applying tools for behavioral change that mattered. And it really had nothing to do with willpower, the elusive little nefarious character we examined in the previous circuit. It had to do with sustained effort of reminding ourselves *why* we were doing this in the first place. In other words, no matter how smart we are, the brain isn't able to focus on more than one thought at a time; therefore, things that we know subconsciously have to be brought to the forefront of our minds before we choose our actions.

One of Dr. Beck's tips that I found most helpful was creating motivation index cards. Each one would contain one reason why I was eating healthier to begin with, and each day (or really anytime I was faced with the short-term challenge of wanting to choose a food that didn't serve me well in the long term) I was supposed to read the cards and then make my food choices. Dr. Beck wanted to empower informed decisions, reminding us of all the reasons why we were on a healthy eating plan to begin with—*before* we went ahead and chose whatever we wanted, whether walking away or digging into the brownie. What I found was promising: all it really took was reading the reminders to make the cravings subside. I didn't need to fight and I didn't need to struggle—I just needed to be reminded. I needed to keep my "whys" close by.

After this, I began making motivation cards for other areas of my life in which I wanted to make better choices, and I found that reading them regularly helped me refocus and strengthen my ability to do better. Reminders are extremely powerful. We might "know" why we are doing something in the back of our mind, we might totally be on board with it in a passive sense, but that is worlds different than focusing on it at the forefront of our attention (which is what the motivation cards force you to do).

I decided to try out a simpler version with my children. Certain young members of our familial cast of characters were in a particularly intense sibling rivalry phase at the time and listening to them argue and cry was becoming rather tiresome. No matter how many times we told them why they should stop fighting and try to get along, it was just not helping in a practical sense. That's when I started hanging up "family buzz words" around the house, which I conceptualized as a simplified form of motivation cards. I worked them into conversation as much as possible: terms like "loyalty," "commitment," "work ethic," "patience," "acceptance." The results for us over time were encouraging.

Mottos are a bit longer and can be a similarly powerful tool. They can refocus us in an instant, remind us what's important, and realign us with our values. Presented again and again, a motto can shift our thinking and norms, connecting brain synapses that will bring them more readily to mind when we need them. For children, buzzwords can be just as powerful. When there are certain concepts we want planted in our children's heads, just exposing them to the words over and over imbues them in their consciousness. Once there, they can hopefully germinate when our children later find themselves in a situation in which we would want them to choose a desired mode of response. Try it at home—whatever it is that's important to you, make sure you mention those words at least once a week.

As parents, we create our children's realities and vocabularies when they are young. Think of baby's first words, and the interesting sayings we hear toddlers voice as they get older. They mimic what they have heard from their parents! Why would it be any different with internal language? How we talk to our children becomes their internal dialogue, and the terms we often use become their inner vocabulary. So, speak often about loyalty, kindness, and love, and the concepts will be more readily at their fingertips. Every family has some differences in what is important to them, but let your children know your family's "whys": Why do we keep Torah and mitzvos? Why is it better to get along with our siblings? Why do we put emphasis on some things over others? Teaching children your family buzzwords from a young age is a short-term investment in the children getting along better day-to-day, a medium-term investment in good interpersonal family relationships, and a long-term investment in your family legacy. And so, keep those whys close by, as the vocabulary of a household ultimately writes the story of your family.

Where to Begin: Takeaways and Tips

🗩 Discussion Starters

- Talk to your children about their "whys" in an effort to motivate and keep focus on whatever they are working on. For older children, help them dig deeper by asking "why?" to their whys.
- Talk to your children about your family's "whys": Why do we keep Torah and mitzvos? Why is it better to get along with our siblings? Why do we put emphasis on some things over others?

➡ Ready for Action

- Help your children make motivation cards for situations that need motivation reminders.
- Decide on some family buzz words and start using them more often; even try posting them around your house.

CHAPTER 17

Circuit 12: Inoculation of Failure

"Failure is one of the greatest gifts bestowed on the faithful."

Rabbi Lord Jonathan Sacks

"I have not failed. I've just found ten thousand ways that won't work."

Thomas A. Edison

Many of us are guilty of "helicopter parenting," a colloquial term that has come to signify overbearing parents who try to control their children's surroundings and intervene in their every problem. The paradox with this method is that when we maelstrom our chopper wings in an effort to sweep all things away that have the potential to make our children feel bad, we are actually doing them a disservice. If we keep our children from failing, we are ultimately setting them up for failure itself. Failure has some benefits, especially in childhood, as children are learning to navigate the world; ultimately, the sooner we learn how to fall, the sooner we learn how to pick ourselves up. The sooner we learn to pick ourselves up, the sooner we learn to dust ourselves off and move on with our lives. And the sooner we move on with our lives after failure rears its ugly head, the sooner happiness returns.

Paul Tough describes the problem well in a *New York Times* magazine piece entitled "What if the Secret to Success Is Failure?" He explains: "We have an acute, almost biological impulse to provide for our children, to give them everything they want and need, to protect them from dangers and discomforts both large and small. And yet we all know—on some level, at least—that what kids need more than anything is a little hardship: some challenge, some deprivation that they can overcome, even if just to prove to themselves that they can. As parents, we struggle with these thorny questions every day, and if we make the right call even half the time, we're lucky. But it's one thing to acknowledge this dilemma in the privacy of our own homes; it's quite another to have it addressed in public, at a school where we send our kids at great expense..."

He goes on to describe educators in the New York City school system who are trying to create "grit" in young students, which as we spoke about in circuit 5, is the toughness and determination that comes after adversity. Dominic Randolph, Head of School at Riverdale Country School, an exclusive private school in the Bronx where they have experimented with teaching children character traits rather than just academics, states: "The idea of building grit and building self-control is that you get that through failure. And in most highly academic environments in the United States, no one fails anything." Tough says that these educators want students to succeed, of course—it's just that they believe that in order to do so, they first need to learn how to fail. And one of the main problems they encounter is parents getting in the way of this. Tough describes educators reporting that they "see many parents who, while pushing their children to excel, also inadvertently shield them from exactly the kind of experience that can lead to character growth." As Fierst (one of the educators) put it: "Our kids don't put up with a lot of suffering. They don't have a threshold for it. They're protected against it quite a bit. And when they do get uncomfortable, we hear from their parents. We try to talk to parents about having to sort of make it O.K. for there to be challenges, because that's where learning happens."

Judaism does not shy away from challenges, even though the very nature of a challenge means that we are opening ourselves up for potential failures. In fact, through our life's challenges, we are told that we will grow, refine ourselves, and according to some, even achieve our purpose in life. As the *Ramchal* states in the *Mesilas Yesharim* (The Path of the Just), one of the main purposes of life is actually to confront a series of challenges that are given to us each individually.[1] The *Orchos Tzaddikim* takes this even a step further when he writes: "Troubles are for the long-term benefit of the individual. As it says: 'Rejoice not against me, my enemy; for when I fall, I will get up; when I sit in darkness, Hashem is light to me.' Our Rabbis of blessed memory taught us, 'If I had fallen, I would not have picked myself up. If I did not sit in darkness, I could not have seen the light.'"

As adults, we know that life is full of challenges and sometimes things don't go our way. Sooner or later, our children will be in on the secret as well. What happens when the harness of childhood has been wrapped so tightly around them? Seems to me that the fall will hurt even more once the harness inevitably goes away and they enter the "real world."

What emerges from this is that we simply can't always intervene to fix our children's problems. As painful as it is to sit back and watch, we need to let them sort through failures on their own. This could mean not writing their papers or doing their homework for them (which unfortunately many parents seem to be doing), not calling the school every time there is a small complaint, and not interfering too much with their friendships when feelings get hurt. As a parent, it's very hard to step back, but try not to get too worked up if children have a little difficulty. We can be there to pick up the pieces and help them learn from the experience, and we can also be their cheerleader, rooting them on to get back up and persevere.

Children can handle more than we think. A bit of overcoming obstacles and facing problems in childhood inoculates them for adulthood, where an understanding of the world as a place where we are supposed to be working on ourselves and overcoming *nisyonos* (tests) is important. Adult life is not full of having fun and getting everything our way.

---

1   "We thus derive that the essence of a man's existence in this world is solely the fulfilling of mitzvos, the serving of God and the withstanding of trials" (*Mesilas Yesharim*, ch. 1).

To bring in the reminder from *Mishlei* again: "כִּי־שֶׁבַע יִפּוֹל צַדִּיק וָקָם"—A righteous person falls seven times but gets up." We can teach our children to not take the first blow as the knockout punch.

No one is saying not to protect our children from larger dangers or failures, or even easily prevented failures as well. By all means do all that you can to help them, but sometimes this might mean letting them fail, in order to learn how to deal with and manage the adversity. Ultimately, we are our children's safety nets—just make sure that net is not pulled so tight that it's a harness, or worse yet a straitjacket.

Where to Begin: Takeaways and Tips

💬 Discussion Starters

- Talk over everyone's thoughts on the *pasuk* in *Mishlei*, "כִּי שֶׁבַע יִפּוֹל צַדִּיק וָקָם" at the dinner table.
- Talk to your children about your own failures in life and how you got through them (or even how they made you stronger, if that was the case).
- Talk to them about mistakes being a perfectly acceptable part of life and that people rarely achieve success without challenges and setbacks. Tell them stories of famous people or *rabbanim* that had setbacks and pushed through (such as the *Netziv*, who admitted to not paying much attention to his studies when he was young. When he was eleven, he overheard his parents planning to pull him out of cheder due to his poor performance, and enroll him to become a shoemaker. Alarmed, he redoubled his efforts to succeed and became the incredible scholar and author of many important commentaries and *sefarim*). There are many such encouraging stories.

➡ Ready for Action

- Let your child get a bad grade, lose the sports game, not get the part they wanted in the school play or class presentation (if these were warranted of course) without calling the school or meddling. The key is to help them get through the pain of that disappointment, and for both of you to achieve being comfortable with being a bit uncomfortable in these situations.

- Pick how many times you will remind your children about something and then don't go beyond it. No one likes being a nag, nor should you have to be one. Give your set number of reminders if needed, and then step back and let your children rise to the occasion. In other words, if you have reminded them three times to put their homework in their backpack and they still don't, it's O.K. to let them lose those points so they will be more motivated next time to either heed your warning, or better yet, be responsible on their own.

- Don't rush to school or camp with nonessential items forgotten at home. Just because you can fix something doesn't mean you should. So if your children forget lunchboxes, signed tests, sneakers for gym, snow pants for recess, treats they were supposed to bring for the class celebration, or anything else they want you to come to the rescue with, try telling them you love them but can't bring it over (short of something for a bodily need like medicine or a change of underwear which, of course, needs to be rushed over). The consequences they will face will probably be small, but will likely help cure forgetfulness.

⚒ Tools

- Move from rescue mode to empowerment mode: Focus on setting your children up for success with remembering the things they need. Instead of running their items to school, make a calendar to keep by the front door that lists the supplies they'll need on different days of the week. Have them keep their backpacks next to the table during homework time so they remember to put their work away.

Or alternatively, leave five minutes before bedtime as the grace period to think over anything they might need for tomorrow that they've forgotten to pack up, so they are not pressured in the morning when they are less likely to remember.

Reinforcement

- Build up confidence in your children's capabilities. Give them direct compliments when they remember something that they usually forget, or achieve a good grade on a paper without your involvement.
- Think back to that look of pride they had as toddlers when they were tenacious and accomplished something for the first time on their own. Consider making a "Proud" badge they can wear in the house when they are feeling good about something they accomplished independently.

CHAPTER 18

Circuit 13:
When Please Isn't So Pretty:
Tackling Vulnerability

*"Corresponding to four sons did the Torah
speak...one is the child who does not know how
to ask."*

Haggadah

*"Vulnerability is the core of shame and fear and
struggle for worthiness, but it appears that it's
also the birthplace of joy."*

Brené Brown

One of my children has mastered the art of "hocking," an extreme form of asking for something repeatedly. Specifically, there is nothing too small or too large that she won't ask for in a given day. It is as if her mind is directly hardwired to her mouth, and the minute something pops in her brain, it doesn't go through the traditional trifold filtering process of:

- "Is this reasonable to ask for?"
- "Is this the right time to ask for it?"
- "Is it worth asking for?"

Now, while this can be completely exhausting for her regular ask-ees (i.e., me and my husband), it has occurred to me that there is a certain rawness in what she is doing that she seems almost immune to. In other words, despite the number of things she asks for and the inevitable ratio of noes it produces, she does not appear in any way dissuaded or hurt by the sheer quantity of rejection that had it been poison, could have killed an elephant by now.

In her book *The Art of Asking*, Amanda Palmer explains that asking makes us vulnerable, and puts us out there in a way that makes us need to be O.K. with getting rejected. We have been socialized to run from vulnerability as much as possible. Therefore, most people shy away from it, saving their "asks" only for when absolutely necessary.

But vulnerability does not have to be bad; asking, with effort, can be an area in which we work on our vulnerability tolerance. In fact, an ask is a connection. It gives the other person an opportunity to forge a bond with us that without the vulnerability would not have been the same. Think about all the people who came through when you asked something of them and reflect—didn't you feel a stronger connection to them after that experience of having "needed" them? And on the flip side, once you went out of your way to help someone or do something that they asked, didn't you feel more invested in the welfare of that other person? Knowing how and when to ask, and more generally, allowing yourself to be vulnerable with others, has been linked to increased happiness.[1]

Asking is a daily part of *tefillah* (prayers); our reliance on Hashem and ability to ask Him with our whole hearts for what we need is a big training ground for both our connection to the Almighty as well as our acceptance of vulnerability. The *Kitzur Shulchan Aruch* codifies that ideally, a *chazzan* for the *Yamim Noraim* (High Holidays) should have children.[2] I have heard it stated that the idea behind this is because those who have children know what it's like to feel vulnerable; it is the awareness of the

---

1 Brené Brown, author of *Daring Greatly: How the Courage to Be Vulnerable Transforms the Way We Live, Love, Parent, and Lead*.
2 *Kitzur Shulchan Aruch, Hilchos Yamim Noraim.*

awesome responsibility for the delicate creations placed into their care that leads to heartfelt *tefillos*."

There are many famous "asks" in *Tanach*, some of which worked out better than others:

- Moshe Rabbeinu's major request to save the Jewish People after the sin of the Golden Calf. He put his whole legacy on the line to do so.
- Avraham's request to save the people of Sodom, and the ensuing negotiations.
- Dovid HaMelech begging Hashem, "אַחַת שָׁאַלְתִּי מֵאֵת ה' אוֹתָהּ אֲבַקֵּשׁ—I have only one thing to ask of You,"[3] where he proceeds to ask to sit in the house of God all of his days. It's one ask, but boy is it a big one.

Then there are some asks where opinions in *Chazal* wish the asker had been bolder. An example of this is Rabbi Yochanan Ben Zakkai asking for Yavneh instead of Jerusalem when Vespasian gave him a genie-like offer to grant one request before the destruction of the Beis Hamikdash (Holy Temple).

Each of these asks teach us a different lesson about asking.

Two skills that people who are more comfortable with being vulnerable learn to excel at are those of asking and saying no. As our children grow older (and more vulnerable), asking actually gets a bit harder for them, given the heightened fear of rejection. We can then help them understand that external factors, such as paying attention to context and surrounding cues, can play an important role in getting a yes. I call this time and place; asking in the wrong context (time) or wrong place can lead to an avoidable no, if only the person had just waited. I've communicated this many times to my darling hocker. When she asks for something while I'm cooking dinner, it might be the right place (our house), but it's definitely the wrong time (while I am octopus-ing between the stove, fridge, pot drawer, and dishwasher all at once). Or say, for example, I've already communicated to her that it's not a great

---

3   *Tehillim* 27:4.

week to have Shabbos playdates over, and she nonetheless brings her friend over to me in shul to plead for plans. It might be the right time (her friend will need the plans set up now because we can't call her later that afternoon) but it's certainly not the right place (always better to ask your mother in private before you suggest an invite, especially one that she is probably going to say no to).

After I have to say no in one of these situational hocking have-to's, I try to debrief with her later on, when we are back in a proper time and place zone. I go over which of the two contexts she missed. It's gotten to the point where instead of having to say a terse no and then going through the back and forth dual of "why not?" I just smile warmly at her, say "time and place," and she realizes it wasn't the right time or perhaps location for the ask. Usually the request is tabled, if not eliminated completely.

Asking is just one piece of vulnerability, but it leads us into the larger issue: Life is messy. We can either embrace the chaos and lean into the discomfort, or run from it and pretend it's not there. Brené Brown, who is a famous researcher on the emotions of shame and vulnerability, explains that at the core of these emotions is the fear of other people disconnecting from us: *Is there something about me that if other people know it or see it, will make me unworthy of connection?* When we worry that maybe if we ask for something (for example, extra explaining from the teacher about a concept that didn't make sense to us), or admit to feeling negative emotions (anger, anxiety, depression), people will think we are "not enough," this keeps us back from being our authentic selves.

Brown explains that the original definition of the word "courage" was "telling the story of who you are with your whole heart." Courage thereby described people who were willing to let go of who they thought they should be and embrace who they actually were. It described people who were willing to embrace vulnerability, not as being comfortable, but as being necessary.

"The people who have a strong sense of love and belonging believe they are worthy of love and belonging," says Brown, "and the ones who don't have it [the strong sense of love and belonging], don't [believe they are worthy]."

We can teach our children that there are many things in life that are neither good nor bad, but instead just are what they are. And one of those is how we struggle. All people struggle because we are hardwired for it,[4] but instead of being ashamed, we can just understand and even embrace it as a regular part of life.

Brown says that we shouldn't look at our children and think, "You're perfect and my job is to keep you perfect," or worse yet, "You are imperfect, and I have to make sure no one finds out." Our job is to acknowledge that our children are imperfect and are wired for struggle, and yet we need to convey to them that they are worthy of love and belonging no matter what these struggles might be.

Teaching our children how to be vulnerable frees them up to be their true selves. Learning to speak up and ask for their needs and wants properly is a great place to start. Ultimately, being comfortable with being our authentic selves is a lifelong skill we need to keep in our toolbox to combat feelings of unworthiness. When honed properly, it can bring us a powerful sense of joy.

Where to Begin: Takeaways and Tips

💬 Discussion Starters

- Talk to your children about the traditional trifold filtering process they should consider before an ask:
  - "Is this reasonable to ask for?"
  - "Is this the right time to ask for it?"
  - "Is it worth asking for?"
- Talk to them about how "no" is a necessary part of life and how to gracefully accept "no" as an answer.

---

4   Brené Brown, "The Power of Vulnerability," filmed June 2010, TED video, https://bit.ly/2GL1mOj.

- Tell your children the following mantra as much as possible: "You are worthy of love and connection."

➲ Ready for Action

- Here is some advice we can teach our children about the recipe of a good "ask":
  - You actually have to *ask* (don't expect people to read your mind). It's best to learn this early.
  - Be direct, clear, and specific about what you want.
  - Know *why* you want it and be ready to articulate that why.
- Practice "time and place" respectful asking.
- Help your children look more deeply at what makes them feel angry, sad, self-conscious, or annoyed, and find the common thread between these experiences. Once you identify these vulnerabilities, you can start to accept and even counter them.
- For older children, try to help them identify their avoidance tactics when they are feeling vulnerable. Do they use food as an escape? Do they try to find an excuse to skip school?

CHAPTER 19

Circuit 14:
The Complain Drain

"תֹּלֶה אֶרֶץ עַל בְּלִימָה"—*The entire world is held up by someone who swallows his response/complaint.*"

Chullin 89a on Iyov 26:7

"What consumes your mind controls your life."

Anonymous

We all have complainers in our lives—in fact, some may be living in our very own bodies! A thorough unloading of our woes from time to time is definitely cathartic, just like a good cry can be very healthy. The issue is when the complaining almost becomes our "go-to" way to unwind, de-stress, or even to start a conversation. I once heard in a *shiur* that part of the punishment given to women after the sin of Chavah is that women sometimes use complaining to make a connection with their spouses, and yet husbands take this as a censure on the life they are providing for their family (*"If she has **this** much to complain about, I'm really doing a crummy job"*).

And then there are those children who seem to find fault in everything. I have one child who is definitely my most prone to complaining, and they managed to complain about everything they encountered one morning (the clothes I put out to wear, the breakfast I placed on the table, the weather prediction, reflections on the day before, how high it was to the top cabinet where the candy was hidden). By the time this child left for camp, you'd think the world was ending—toppled not by war, hatred, and sickness, but by the wrong-colored shirt and limited access to the gumballs. I felt completely drained and began to wonder how exactly this child felt. Was he or she miserable after leveling all this criticism, or did the child feel better after unearthing these great injustices and declaring them to the world?

"Everyone complains, at least a little," says Dr. Robin Kowalski, a professor of psychology at Clemson University. But Kowalski goes on to explain that not all complaining was created equal. She categorizes complainer types as the *venters*, the *sympathy seekers*, and the *chronic complainers*:

- The **venter** is a "dissatisfied person who doesn't want to hear solutions, however brilliant."
- The **sympathy seekers** thrive on proving that they have it worse than the rest of their peers or just are more gloom-and-doom folks. These people need the jolt of sympathy for their own happiness, and find it's often quickly generated by complaining.
- The **chronic complainers** do something researchers call "ruminating." This means they are basically stuck in a mental loop of focusing on their problems, worrying about them, and feeling the need to talk about them. The problem with this group is that instead of feeling a release or burst of comfort and joy after complaining, they actually feel worse because once they reopen the issue, it can rocket them back into the mental loop of agonizing all over again. This can then lead to even more worry and anxiety.

B'nei Yisrael has historically not been immune to complaining either. The Torah has many stories of famous complaints, ranging from Korach who claimed to be rallying against communal injustice, to the *misonenim ra* ("kvetchers") who, *Chazal* tell us, didn't even know what they were complaining about. Even the *meraglim* (spies), who thought they knew what they were complaining about, were judged as creating an outcry for no reason, making that day (Tishah B'Av) eternally auspicious for crying.

Research shows that most people complain once a minute during a typical conversation.[1] Complaining is tempting because it feels good, but like many other things that bring a temporary boost, complaining isn't good for us and might even become addictive.

Throughout our lives, we wire our brains based on our repetitive thinking. We get good at what we practice. Our brain loves efficiency and doesn't like to work any harder than it has to. When we repeat a response like complaining, our neurons branch out to each other to ease the flow of information. This makes it much easier to complain the next time we are in a similar situation, and as we keep repeating this response it can become almost second nature to us. The next thing we know, complaining can become our "default mode."

If our internal sound track is self-criticism, worries, and how nothing is working out for us, our minds will more easily find that track in our brains and replay those same thoughts again. It assumes they are on our "favorites mix" when we encounter a stressor or something that throws us off kilter. This makes us more vulnerable to anxiety, as our internal cassette tape starts to unravel.

There are other neurological underpinnings of why complaining can become addictive. When we complain, our bodies release the stress hormone cortisol, which shifts us into fight-or-flight mode, directing oxygen, blood, and energy away from everything except the systems that are essential to immediate survival.

According to Dr. Travis Bradberry, coauthor of *Emotional Intelligence 2.0*, "Since human beings are inherently social, our brains naturally and unconsciously mimic the moods of those around us, particularly people we spend a great deal of time with. This process is called *neuronal mirroring*, and it's the basis for our ability to feel empathy. The flip side, however, is that it makes complaining a lot like smoking—you don't have to do it yourself to suffer the ill effects."[2]

Dr. Bradberry recommends several solutions to combat complaining. First off, when the urge hits you to complain, try to shift your

---

1   https://www.entrepreneur.com/article/281734.
2   https://bit.ly/2ZnQHzz.

attention to something that you're grateful for. Bradberry says that taking the time to contemplate what we're grateful for can reduce the stress hormone cortisol by twenty-three percent. He goes on to cite research conducted at the University of California which found that people who worked daily to cultivate an attitude of gratitude experienced improved mood, energy, and substantially less anxiety due to lower cortisol levels. Not to mention the fact that our brains can't actually think two things at once. Therefore, if we are focusing on gratitude, we can't simultaneously be annoyed and trigger-happy to launch the next complaint.

The next strategy Dr. Bradberry recommends is that when we do need to complain, we should try to do so in a solution-oriented way. He breaks this down into four components:

1. **Have a clear purpose.** Know what your goal is before you start complaining. If you can't identify a way the problem can be fixed by bringing it up, then there's a good chance you just want to complain for the sake of complaining. This is what we are trying to avoid.

2. **Start with something positive.** It may seem counterintuitive, but starting with a positive statement helps keep the other person from getting defensive. For example, you can tell your child, "Before you launch into your list of complaints about everything that went wrong in school today, please tell me something positive that happened."

3. **Be specific.** When you're complaining, it's not a good time to make sweeping statements about how people "always are," or bring up every minor peccadillo from the past decade. Just address the current situation and be as specific as possible. Teach your children that instead of making general statements such as, "I hate my teacher, she is always mean to me," just say the specific example of what the teacher did that day and why your child felt it was mean.

4. **End on a positive.** Think about an adult scenario for this one. Dr. Bradberry says that if you end your complaint with, "I'm

never shopping here again," the person who's listening has no motivation to act on your complaint. In that case, you're just venting, or complaining with no purpose. Instead, restate your purpose, as well as your hope that the desired result can be achieved. For example, "I'd like to work this out so that we can keep our business relationship intact." With our children this might look like shifting them from generalizations such as, "I'm never going to school again!" to "I really want to figure out how to make school happier so I actually want to go again."

Try to catch your internal complaining and negative thoughts before they become words. We don't want to give our children the second-hand smoke effect of lowering their moods, and worse yet, modeling the addictive loop of complaining. Some of us are born to complain and some have it thrust upon us, but both ultimately end up feeling "complain drain." The weather may be bad, your house might be a perennial mess, your finances may be in the toilet, and the candy might be too high for you to reach, but all you need to do is close your eyes, be grateful for the good, and have your brain transport you anywhere with a one-seater available for one thought at a time...

Where to Begin: Takeaways and Tips

⟴ Ready for Action

- Try a seven-day "no complaining" family challenge and see what its effects are on the mood at home.
- If you have to complain or vent to someone, try to not do it in front of your children.
- Practice more gratitude.

📖 Teachable Moment

- When you catch your children complaining, try to channel it into solution-oriented complaining using Dr. Bradberry's four components. If you catch them complaining for no reason, talk to them about how they can make it productive to find a solution, rather than just speaking negatively with no purpose.

Reinforcement

- Make awards for difficult situations that your family might usually complain about but managed not to (long road trips, meals that they don't like, a visit to a home with no toys).

CHAPTER 20

Circuit 15:
Sleep for Happiness

*"Sleep is one of the necessary blessings of life,
allowing a person to refresh one's body and spirit."*

Rabbi Berel Wein

*"Without enough sleep we all become tall
two-year-olds."*

Jojo Jensen

Humans are the *only* species on the planet who will deprive themselves of sleep. Shows how smart *we* are.

Sleep promotes growth, helps the heart, battles germs, affects weight, reduces risk of injury, increases attention spans, and boosts learning. Sleep is when the body repackages neurotransmitters, which are the communication chemicals of brain cells, and also when our brain cells "take out the trash" each night, flushing away disease-causing toxins (and when some of us forget to take out the real trash from the kitchen).

To directly address our central topic, studies have found sleep to even be the most important factor in happiness.

The 2017 BTN Happiness Survey[1] involving forty-seven thousand Australian children found that getting enough sleep was the biggest

---

1   Conducted by the University of Melbourne and *Behind the News* TV program.

reported indicator of their happiness and made children twice as likely to report feeling happy. A recent Gallup poll produced the same findings in adults: People who get adequate sleep are more likely to rate their lives as happier.[2]

The flip side has also been proven: Eighty-eight percent of parents reported that their child's overall mood was impacted without quality sleep, and eighty-one percent reported their child's performance in school was affected by the amount of sleep they got. Studies out of the University of Binghamton and University of California, Berkeley have shown that people who don't get enough sleep experience more repetitive negative thoughts and the emotional centers of their brains run amok. The more telling finding in the University of Binghamton study though, was that this was also true of subjects who got "enough" sleep, but got it later at night, suggesting that the timing of sleep also plays a critical role. In other words, you might want to tread lightly around those night owls in your inner circle.

For children, sleep can be even more important for behavior and impulse control because many areas of the brain that control these processes are not as developed as they are in adults. Studies have shown that parents who put their children to bed an hour earlier every night for a week already saw improvement in their children's behavior.[3]

Napping has been shown to be very beneficial as well. According to a study out of the University of Pennsylvania, children who nap thirty to sixty minutes midday at least three times a week are happier, have more self-control and grit, and showcase fewer behavioral problems. These children also have higher IQs and excel academically. The most surprising part of this study is that they were talking about children aged ten to twelve![4]

---

2   Gallup-Healthways Well-Being Index.

3   Avi Sadeh, Reut Gruber, and Amiram Raviv, "The Effects of Sleep Restriction and Extension on School-Age Children: What a Difference an Hour Makes," *Child Development* 74, no. 2 (2003): 444–55.

4   Jianghong Liu, Rui Feng, Xiaopeng Ji, Naixue Cui, Adrian Raine, and Sara C. Mednick, "Midday napping in children: Associations between nap frequency and duration across

Drowsiness affects up to twenty percent of all children, says lead author on the study Jianghong Liu. What's more, the negative cognitive, emotional, and physical effects of poor sleep habits are well-established, and yet most people in America only see a value in napping their children until preschool age. While we can't go around changing our immediate cultural surroundings, in many other parts of the world such as China, a midday break is normal and often even adults nap during this time.

Between twenty and thirty percent of children have experienced sleep problems, says Dr. Jodi Mindell. This can include sleepwalking, night terrors, and insomnia. Some issues—like snoring—may seem harmless, but could actually be a sign of a major concern like sleep apnea or a lesser concern like poor quality of sleep. In our family, every single one of my children has had their tonsils and adenoids removed as a result of snoring and poor sleep concerns (we call it "Perkel nose syndrome").

The repercussions of sleep deprivation can be seen after four consecutive nights missing only one hour each night. This can easily happen during Chol Hamoed, when company sleeps over, or especially during the summer months. "I expected that we'd see some differences when kids get less sleep than usual," says senior author Penny Corkum, PhD, in one of the studies that discovered this phenomenon. "But finding that they're so drastically affected in so short an amount of time is amazing."

Many families also find that once they have older kids, it's much harder to get their younger kids to sleep at an early hour. The problem with this is that younger children really do need more sleep, and therefore benefit from being in bed earlier. It is important to set boundaries—in other words, just like we don't let our younger children have the same privileges as our older children (walking in the neighborhood alone, using knives to cut food), we can explain that they are also not old enough to have the privilege of a late bedtime. Below is a chart that shows how much sleep is recommended for various ages. To calculate the right bedtime, just subtract these numbers from the time you need

---

cognitive, positive psychological well-being, behavioral, and metabolic health outcomes," *Sleep*, 2019.

your children to get up in the morning (and pad it with an extra fifteen minutes to half hour to allow for bedtime routine).

National Sleep Foundation Recommendations for Sleep per Age

Age of Child	Hours of Sleep Needed (at least)
3–12 months	9.5 to 14 hours
1–3 years	12 to 14 hours
3–5 years	11 to 13 hours
5–12 years	10 to 11 hours
12–19 years	8 to 10 hours

Some ways to improve our children's sleep:

- **Encourage self-soothing at any age.** I have a child mid-elementary school who still often finds me at night "to say hi" when waking up to use the bathroom. This often involves traipsing through levels of the house where the lights are still on, and it is clearly a bad habit formed from earlier childhood. I gently remind this child that it's not good for their sleep cycle to wake up the brain with lights, and that they are perfectly capable of tucking themselves back in after a bathroom trip.
- **Work on making sure your child feels safe and secure in your relationship with them.** Many a child has stayed up worrying that their parent is angry at them or doesn't love them anymore. Find ways to give your child a little personal attention before bed (a kind word, bedtime book, saying *Shema*, tucking them in, patting their head) and try not to let them go to sleep with an unresolved fight between you. Studies have shown that children who feel more secure sleep better.
- **Have a regular bedtime routine.** Set bedtimes that are consistent with the amount of sleep your children need and use the above

chart to calculate. Develop a routine that provides a sense of pre-
dictability that bedtime is about to come, priming their bodies for
sleep. A relaxing shower, a quiet cuddle while reading, and a brief
pillow-chat about their day are all good ideas. "Of all activities,
reading printed books appears to be most relaxing," says Michael
Gradisar, a clinical psychologist at Flinders University.

- **Ensure your child gets enough physical activity during the day
  to tire them out.** Moving our bodies not only does the obvious
  job of burning up physical energy, but it is also positively associated with the brain chemistry people need to manage stress and
  sleep well. While many Jewish schools have outdoor recess, they
  are often lacking in sufficient gym classes. This trend, coupled
  by longer hours for dual curriculums, means that many of our
  children are not getting enough time each day to run around.
  Try to encourage more movement at home or tailor after-school
  activity choices to promote more exercise.

- **Reduce exposure to technology two hours before bed.** The
  blue light that comes out of technology devices messes with our
  circadian rhythms and can make our brains feel that there is
  daylight (even during the night). This interferes with our brains
  registering that it is actually dark and time for sleep. Try to
  avoid your child playing a game on your phone or typing up their
  homework essay right before bed, as this can actually mess with
  their ability to fall asleep.

- **Make sure their fears are dealt with.** If something is bothering
  them, it will often pop into their heads at night when they are
  alone and have nothing else to think about. There was a murder of
  a Jewish *bachur* near our neighborhood one Simchas Torah night.
  While I would have never dreamed of talking about this with my
  then sensitive six-year-old, we happened to be at a restaurant a
  few days later and the people eating next to us were talking about
  the details quite loudly. It scared my daughter, and after this she
  had several months of bad sleep resulting from nighttime fear.
  We tried our best during the day to talk about the worries and
  deal with them to make night as manageable as possible.

At the end of the day (literally), the time we let ourselves "shut off" makes the time that we are "on" so much more successful. And while we might think of Judaism as downplaying sleep for adults given so many stories of *gedolim* who hardly slept at all, there are actually many sources that back up its import (especially for those of us not on quite as exalted a level). The *Rambam* in *Hilchos Dei'os* says that the right amount of time for sleep is eight hours, and in our times Rav Shach wrote that a person should not have less than six to seven hours of sleep because this can, God forbid, harm their health.

And so, the next time the sun goes down and the house gets quiet with all your normal noisemakers nestled in their beds, do yourself a favor and don't shun the shuteye.

Where to Begin: Takeaways and Tips

💬 Discussion Starters

- Talk your children through fears or family fights during the day so their minds are not ruminating about those difficulties at night.
- Explain to younger children that bedtimes, like other privileges, increase with age and that younger bodies need more sleep in order to feel better.

➡ Ready for Action

- Work on adjusting your kids' bedtimes to make sure they are getting their age-appropriate amounts of sleep (see chart in chapter).
- Work on good sleep habits for the family: low light, calming routine before bed, quiet, and cool temperature in the room during sleep.
- Talk to a doctor about frequent night waking or snoring in children.
- Model good sleep habits yourself.

🛠 Tools

- White noise machines can be very helpful for masking background noise from a bustling family during younger children's bedtimes. If they can't hear what's going on downstairs, they won't feel they are missing out. We own several of these that are portable enough to even take on trips when we don't know how noisy our sleeping arrangements will be.

Environment

CHAPTER 21

Circuit 16:
Filling Our Lives

"How much better is it to acquire wisdom than gold! And to acquire understanding is preferable to silver."

Mishlei 16:16

"Happiness is never found in materialistic things; it exists in things that cannot be physically possessed. Therefore, happiness is priceless. It can never be purchased."

Ellen J. Barrier

There is a story about a fabulously wealthy Orthodox philanthropist who died. He left behind a huge estate, half of which was given to charity and the other half to his children. He also left behind two mysterious letters: one was meant to be opened immediately and the other had explicit instructions to remain sealed until thirty days after his death.

The first letter contained his will, dividing the entire estate among the beneficiaries except for one item: a pair of his favorite socks. Stranger still, he emphatically demanded in the letter that his children bury him in these socks. Attempting to meet their father's last wish, the children immediately brought the socks to the *chevra kadishah* (burial society), and requested that their father be buried in them.

The *chevra kadishah* refused, citing the Jewish law that a person cannot be buried in anything other than the traditional burial shroud. The children were aghast. They explained that besides the fact that their father had been a big supporter of the burial society in his lifetime, he was also a very learned man and would never have made such a request if it could not be fulfilled. But the *chevra kadishah* remained firm in their decision. The family frantically turned to rabbinical authorities, *talmidei chachamim,* and anyone they could think of who could help find a loophole to fulfill their patriarch's dying wish. They got nowhere and with great sorrow, their father was buried without his socks.

When thirty days had passed, with shaking hands and a heavy heart, the eldest brother opened the second letter. It read something like this:

> *My precious children,*
>
> *By now you must have buried me without my socks and by now I hope you understand the message: No matter what a person's material processions are in this world, no matter how many millions of dollars he has, he goes to his Maker naked as the day he was born—just like everybody else. Nothing comes with you to the next world except the deeds from your lifetime…not even your favorite pair of socks.*

This simple story is a great place to start when trying to teach our children how happiness cannot be found in physical items. As we confront the endless pursuit of materialism characterized by the times in which we live, we must seek to undo the damage by sending a different message to our own homes and communities.

Two examples:

- There was a study done in the 1990s of children growing up in low-income families and neighborhoods. One of the astounding findings was that the children didn't even realize they were poor! Because everyone around them was living similar lives with minimal "things" available to them, they didn't realize they were missing out and were actually rather happy. They only became unhappy once they glimpsed the lives of the high-income neighborhood.

- A friend recently sent me a similar story witnessed in her community about a teenage girl who tagged along while her mother shopped for a new *sheitel*. The mother found one that she liked and told the seller that she wanted to purchase it. The *sheitel* seller, knowing that this woman had very little money, gently explained, "This one is quite expensive...why don't I show you some beautiful ones that are in a more affordable price range?" The woman replied, "I can't afford a new *sheitel* to begin with, so what's the difference? As long as I am overextending myself, I may as well have the one that I like." At this point the daughter exclaimed, "Mommy, what are you saying? I didn't realize we were poor!"

How could it be that this girl reached her teenage years without noticing the poverty of her family? My guess is that she grew up in a household that generally didn't put much value on material things, and so she never noticed the lack. And while it's very hard for children to remain sheltered from materialism while growing up in a society where so many people put value on objects, we can at least start to show where we place our values in the home. We can create a happy environment despite "the latest craze." Children might still see the latest and greatest toy, game, and collectible item outside the home, but if they see that they live in a family where people seem to be happy without constantly pursuing those items, then hopefully they will realize that happiness exists from something other than objects.

There is a very powerful Mishnah in *Pirkei Avos* (4:21), where Rabbi Eliezer HaKapar says, "הַקִּנְאָה וְהַתַּאֲוָה וְהַכָּבוֹד מוֹצִיאִין אֶת הָאָדָם מִן הָעוֹלָם—Jealousy, desire, and honor-seeking drive a person from this world." What it is about these three pursuits that literally *remove us* from the world? They don't kill us; a person does not literally die of jealousy, wanting something, or seeking esteem. The answer is that these raw emotions and driving forces literally remove us from the world because of their tendency to be endless pursuits. The pursuit of things we don't have detracts from our enjoyment of what we do have in the here and now. These tendencies can quickly overshadow our happiness because we are no longer looking inward for joy and tranquility; we are instead looking outside of ourselves. In other words, the endless acquisition of things will ultimately be the end of us. This is a great Mishnah to share and discuss with older children.

I am not advocating asceticism. Having toys, new clothes, special serving pieces, and things that we enjoy are a natural part of life. In fact, *Chazal* even encourage new purchases such as these for special times like Yom Tov.

The problem is when we enmesh too much of our happiness with thoughts of what we think we are missing, and this is a red flag we need to be on the watch for with our children. When we see they don't seem to be happy with their current toys, clothes, or objects only because they say they are "sick of them" or "need more," and this becomes a recurring pattern, that is the time to step in and try to help our children learn to disentangle their happiness from their objects.

I have a friend who constantly rotates the presence and availability of the existing toys in her house. In other words, she only keeps a certain amount out and available to play with at a given time so that the ones that are hidden away will seem new again when she takes them out another week. The hidden ones literally become out of sight and out of mind and so they are exciting all over again when they are put back in the rotation and made available. I tried this myself and found that instead of the scaled-back selection of toys limiting my children's creativity as I had previously worried—*Won't they be more creative and happy if they have so many options in front of them to pair together and play with?*—it actually helped them. They focused more attention and joy on what was in front of them, instead of constantly jumping from object to object and ultimately getting bored.

The bottom line is, no matter what the age or pursuit, we can teach our children to find joy beyond the realm of "things." Objects can fill our rooms, but they can never fill up our lives. We can gently explain to our children that everyone sometimes feels loneliness or emptiness, but that void cannot be filled by the latest object; it represents a deeper longing for relationships, purpose, and meaning to fill our *lives*. That can be found in moments, people, and ideas, not in any material item we can purchase. It's a lofty concept, and not always an easy one to grasp, but to change our mindsets we have to start somewhere. And we can certainly start with a little story about favorite socks.

Where to Begin: Takeaways and Tips

▣ Discussion Starters

- Discuss the Mishnah in *Pirkei Avos*, "Jealousy, desire, and honor-seeking drive a person from this world," at the dinner table one night.
- Ask your children if their happiness was ever affected by thoughts of what they think they are missing or don't have?
- Ask your children how long a specific new toy really made them happy before they started thinking about the next one they wanted? Use this as a springboard to talk about how natural it is for human beings to want more, but how much happier they are when they focus on enjoying what they have.

➡ Ready for Action

- Try rotating the presence and availability of the existing toys in your house. See if your children become excited all over again when older toys are put back in the rotation.
- Focus on quality time with you as a reward for your child, versus using an item or treat. For example, participate in a special activity together as the reward.
- Generosity: Take your children to do *chessed* (acts of kindness), and then point out how much their time and efforts meant to the cause. Or have them pick out some items to donate that they have enjoyed but aren't using anymore. Help them write a note giving the next child ideas from

their favorite ways to play with the toy/use the object and wishing the next child lots of joy with it as well.

- Role model contentment with what you have yourself as an adult.

Reinforcement

- Instead of giving "stuff" as a reward, give well-earned compliments that focus on inner qualities. These compliments (and more broadly, increasing self-esteem) have been found to successfully reduce materialistic tendencies.[1]

---

1   L.N. Chaplin and D.R. John, "Growing up in Material World: Age differences in materialism in children and adolescents," *Journal of Consumer Research*, 34, 4 (2007):480–493.

CHAPTER 22

Circuit 17:
Displaying Joy Yourself

"הֶרְגֵּל שֶׁנַּעֲשָׂה טֶבַע שֵׁנִי"—*What you are accustomed*
to do will become your second nature."

Netziv, Ha'amek Davar (Shemos 29:20)

"Fake it 'til you make it."

English aphorism

My precious firstborn, when he was about two years old at the time, and had very few multiword phrases under his belt, blurted out something in the back of the car one day that shocked me. *"Be happy, Ima!"* In his limited lexicon, he had put all his words and thoughts together to convey that message to me. And believe me, he has continued to convey it many times since then when he sensed I was unhappy.

On that fateful first time in the car, I was going through one of life's little rough patches but was confident that I hadn't let him see it. *Or had I?*

The truth is, the nonverbal cues and communication that children pick up on are not to be underestimated. They understand much more than the language of tantrums that they often use to convey their own hard feelings. Longer silences, reduced smiling, general sullenness—children know when adults are not happy—even bright-blue-eyed wispy-haired toddlers, ordering you from their car seat to do a 180-degree turn on your emotions.

135

From that moment forward, I became convinced that one of the most powerful tools to teach children happiness is to show them how we find happiness ourselves. A household as a whole is only as strong as its individual parts, and good modeling is one of the most powerful tools in parenting. This is no exception when it comes to happiness. In other words, if we want our children to be happy, we'd better work on being genuinely happy ourselves. Our behavior, language, reactions, mood, responses, resilience, positivity, and reinforcement all influence how our children will perceive and react to both challenges and successes. Are we destroyed when someone hurts our feelings or do we manage to shake it off with grace? Do we grumble to ourselves and grouch at the people around us when life doesn't go our way, or do we compartmentalize in a way that mitigates the effects of our disappointments on the people around us?

With adult trials and tribulations, modeling can often mean showing children how to be happy *despite* ("This particular thing bothered me, but I am not going to let it ruin my day, week, month, year"). Life is rife with challenges, and better that we offer children a window into seeing how we deal with them, instead of pretending everything is perfect until children are blindsided by the reality that it's not. Even with my seven-year-old and four-year-old, I will say, "Wow, that phone conversation I just had with someone really bothered me, but I'm not going to let it ruin my day," or "When you just had that tantrum it really made me feel upset, but I'm going to work on myself to move past those feelings now that the tantrum is over."

I recently heard that however young children see their parents react to situations will be their default setting for how they initially react to similar situations when they are adults. Even if they develop stronger resiliency than their parents and refine themselves to act upon things differently, their initial gut reaction will be what they saw from childhood. For example, if we as parents get annoyed every time it rains ("I'm so upset, now we can't go have our afternoon outside...what a pain, now there's going to be more traffic...now this is going to ruin my suit, etc.), they will innately feel a triggered sense of annoyance when the droplets become a downpour in the future. While other factors can affect how we react to events, the beginning point is often how our parents reacted.

What I am trying to hone in on here is that the general environment of the household can either make or break a child's level of happiness. The main reason for this is that in childhood, happiness is often inextricably linked to family happiness. And yet, while the environment is critical, this is not to say that we have to run a circus where everyone is happy-clappy all day long. It's more about equilibrium than anything else. Negativity has to sometimes happen: reprimands are necessary in order to teach, and there are inevitable punishments that have to be doled out in order to instruct. Rebbetzin Sima Spetner (a sought-after parenting expert in Israel) teaches parents about a "4:1 ratio" that keeps children feeling happy in a household. What she has found through experience is that over the course of a day or a week, there should be four positive interactions for every one necessary negative interaction. The point of this ratio is to balance out any negative feelings and keep children feeling comfortable and happy. This is a helpful tool for taking stock of whether things in our households are out of whack. And if they are—if we notice that we are giving our children too many commands, reprimands, and punishments, and if there are too many fights erupting—we can either try to reduce these negative interactions or just increase the number of positive ones. We can also do a little of both. Increasing positive interactions could take the form of more hugs, more one-on-one time, more compliments, more pointing out your children's successes to them, and so much more. This can bring the environment back to more comfortable and happy ground.

Unhappy households aren't only stressful for the negative feelings they evoke, but research shows they also make it hard for children to succeed academically. Paul Tough, in his book *How Children Succeed*, says that poor performance in school can sometimes be traced back to unhappy home lives. Tough explains:

> *The part of the brain most affected by early stress is the prefrontal cortex, which is critical in self-regulatory activities of all kinds, both emotional and cognitive. As a result, children who grow up in stressful environments generally find it harder to concentrate, sit still, rebound from disappointments, and follow directions.*

And that has a direct effect on their performance in school. When you're overwhelmed by uncontrollable impulses and distracted by negative feelings, it's hard to learn the alphabet.

No one is always happy, and no family is always happy either. However, we certainly can strive for *happy enough*. With the "4:1 ratio" as a tool for general reflection, and with the knowledge that children are watching us for cues and guidance (taking it all in like funnels without filters), we can be more mindful of our own behaviors and reactions as we push ourselves just a little harder to show happiness. Even during those times when we feel unhappy, don't forget that we can always fake it until we make it. Remember, research shows that people who smile (even fake smiles) feel happier afterward. Personally, I'm sure I flashed a fake one that day at my precious little prince dolling out happiness advice from his car seat in between swigs of his sippy cup.

Where to Begin: Takeaways and Tips

🗩 Discussion Starters

- Talk to older children about compartmentalizing: Just because you are upset about one thing, doesn't mean it needs to ruin your other interactions or parts of your day when you are not having to deal with that particular problem.
- Let your children know when you are choosing to be happy even though something has upset you.

➡ Ready for Action

- Smile at your children more.
- Work on the 4:1 ratio of positive interactions to negative interactions in your home.
- Try to be more cognizant of the language you use to speak about things that are bothering you, keeping in mind that you are teaching your children how to react in those situations.

CHAPTER 23

Circuit 18:
Lose the Rush

"'וַאֲבַדְתֶּם מְהֵרָה' *teaches us to lose the rush.*"

Piaseczna Rav, Kalonymus Kalman Shapira

"You're only here for a short visit. Don't hurry,
don't worry. And be sure to smell the flowers along
the way."

Walter Hagen

Of recent memory, few Talmudic stories have been harder for me
to shake than the story of Alexander the Great at the Gates of Paradise.[1]
Years ago, my husband told it over to my son at dinner one night, and
his inquisitive blue eyes were completely entranced:

> *Alexander the Great alighted to Gates of Gan Eden and banged*
> *on the door, demanding to be let in. He was answered with the*
> *verse from Tehillim (118:20), "This is the Gate of God, only*
> *righteous people may enter." But Alexander was undeterred.*
> *"But I'm a king! They call me 'the Great!' There must be some-*
> *thing you can give me." And so, God did indeed give him some-*
> *thing—a circular object. Not knowing its meaning, Alexander*
> *decided to (literally) weigh its importance in the only way he*

---

1   *Tamid* 32b.

knew how: He put it on one side of the scale and put all his valuable possessions on the other side. No matter how many things from his various conquests he added, the small circular object outweighed them all.

The object was an eyeball. It outweighed every valuable object that Alexander had ever pursued and amassed because no matter what a person does or acquires, the eyeball is never satisfied. You can be a conqueror of nations like Alexander the Great and go around the world, accomplish and acquire everything your eyeball sees, but once the current pursuit is over, that eyeball will still want more.

Shocked, Alexander asked the rabbis to prove to him that the object was an eyeball. They placed dust on it to render its vision useless, and suddenly the scale tilted completely to the side of the riches.

There are many lessons I see in this story. What I want to focus on here is the lesson of what comes from endless conquests, not in terms of objects, but in terms of expended time.

We live in a society where the pace of life is, dare I say, crazy. Most of us run around all day as if someone pressed our fast-forward button. We try to pack in every possible pursuit, experience, and "necessity," and if you are anything like me, you still find that there are very few things that have been checked off your to-do list each day despite this haste.

The same pace of life trickles down to our children: Many are over-scheduled, and this doesn't leave enough downtime for imaginative play and creativity. I have spoken to many parents who are determined to give their kid "every possible opportunity out there," which often translates into way too many after-school programs and activities. As adults in a high-pressured, competitive society, we want to give our children the best possible edge and so we are often made to feel like we have done them a disservice if we haven't provided every support program and/or enrichment out there. But what if the disservice is that we are actually making them feel too much pressure at too young an age?

Many years ago, I attended a lecture by Dr. David Pelcovitz where he mentioned a fascinating homiletical take on the phrase from *Shema*, "וַאֲבַדְתֶּם מְהֵרָה," attributed to the Piaseczna Rav, Kalonymus Kalman Shapira. Normally translated literally as "You will be lost quickly," the homiletical interpretation quoted was an allusion to slowing down the pace of our lives: "Lose the rush!" Putting these literal and nonliteral meanings together I see a message of "lose the rush before the rush makes you lost."

I believe the impediment we sometimes create that can block our children's sense of *menuchas hanefesh* is the pressure of over-scheduling. Downtime and time for creativity and reflection are so important for happiness. And when I say downtime, I am not talking about plugging them in to an electronic device.

The other piece of all this is that children simply don't appreciate being hurried in the first place. They find themselves rushed all the time, not always because *their* schedules make things busy, but because *our* schedules make everything busy. We as parents have very demanding lives and often this translates into rushing our children from place to place. It makes children stressed out to be under the gun of time pressure even more than it stresses us out, and studies show many parents are downplaying or not even realizing the level of their children's stress.[2] The reason for this is because we at least have control over our schedules so we know what is happening next. Children, however, often have no idea what is coming. So suddenly going from being in a world of imaginative play to having to cut it short as they are herded into a car can be quite disorienting and frustrating. Personally, I find it helps so much to let my children know five to ten minutes ahead of time that we are going to need to leave. That way, they can wrap up what they are doing instead of suddenly getting a rush order of "Put on your shoes, get your coat and bag (insert any other object here) now so we can go!"

We used to live in a top floor condo and so the "boarding process" of getting all my children to the car took a good fifteen minutes. We'd have

---

2   https://bit.ly/32caIdX; https://bit.ly/2RbwfgN.

to do all the usual "gearing up" of proper clothing and footwear, gathering what we needed to take with, getting out the door and all the way down the long condo hall to the elevator, waiting sometimes for up to several minutes for it to make it to our floor, taking the elevator all the way down to the underground garage and then walking to our distant parking space…and all this before we ever laid eyes on the actual car.

No matter how many times I went through this process, my brain simply could not comprehend why it took a quarter of an hour. As a result, I'd ultimately reach my car in a state of shock, annoyance, and extreme lateness—none of which are ingredients for success. Once we clambered in, my then three-year-old son would ultimately throw a fit about wanting to independently buckle himself into his car seat (another numerous-minute process) and by then I would lose it. "We don't have time—it took too long to get downstairs yet again. Let's *go*." One day, as he struggled with his small fingers to maneuver the web of car seat buckles likely complicated enough to be NASA spacecraft-grade safety compliant, he turned to me and sternly said, "You are always rushing me and it makes me feel bad." I stopped immediately mid-frustration, let him take as much time as he needed, and made it a point to leave our condo five to ten minutes earlier from then on. By that small shift in our schedule I set myself up for success (also a Rebbetzin Spetner phrase) so that no matter what, I had that extra five minutes to let him fumble with the car seat to his heart's content. That small move to leave the rush behind us made a sizable difference in his going off to school happy, feeling like he had accomplished his desired task independently that morning.

As it says in *Koheles* (1:8), "The eye is never sated with seeing." There is always more to do and pursue. That is the nature of existence. Lose the rush, though, and you'll begin to see how much you gain. Pick a few things to pursue for your children's enrichment, development, and even entertainment, but don't try to do it all. Try to slow down the pace of your family life, even if it means waking up ten minutes earlier to make the epic morning preparations for leaving the house smoother. Or tell your children the list of that whole day's schedule so they know *what* will be expected of them *when* and *where*, so they won't feel so rushed.

At some point, all our eyeballs will be covered with dust and we too will be knocking on the door of Gan Eden. Let us learn from Alexander the Not-So-Great's mistakes, and not forget that while we are here on this earth, endless pursuits are not necessarily the best end in and of themselves.

Where to Begin: Takeaways and Tips

➔ **Ready for Action**

- Go through your daily schedule and see where the pace can be slowed down.
- Consider waking up earlier to ease some of the morning rush.
- Try not to overschedule your children with after-school activities and commitments.
- Try giving your children a head's up of the Shabbos or Sunday schedule (with approximate times they will need to leave the house) so they aren't surprised when they are suddenly told to get ready to leave.
- Try the technique of "setting yourself up for success" by leaving extra time for tasks that take your children longer than you might ideally want them to (but is the current reality).
- If you are someone who chronically runs late, this can be very stressful to your kids. For the next two weeks, try to leave five to ten minutes earlier than usual so you don't feel road rage and/or commute stress (even if this means getting there a few minutes early). See whether this reduces the family stress level.

CHAPTER 24

Circuit 19:
Visual Happiness

*"Three things ease one's mind...[the first one is] a
beautiful dwelling..."*

Talmud, Berachos 57b

*"Rooms should not be put together for show but to
nourish one's well-being."*

Albert Hadley

I never knew that my husband hated the color green until I inno-
cently painted half the house that very color.

As I mentioned in an earlier chapter, several years ago, we bought a
"fixer-upper" and, well, majorly fixed it up. My husband, a very easygo-
ing guy with absolutely no interest in home decorating, was more than
happy to give me *carte blanche* in picking everything for the project. In
deciding the colors for the rooms, I had a little too much fun. Inspired
by many colors that I admired in other houses, I couldn't help but put
them all in our own. This ended up manifesting in everything from gold
paint in the dining room to an orange russet color in the laundry room.
And did I mention, green, green, and more green? Sea-foam green for
the guest room, turquoise for our master bedroom (I called that blue,
but apparently, he saw it as green), and as a crowning-green-glory, my
one-year-old daughter's bedroom in eye-popping neon green. I saw

the neon green as a happy, vibrant color, radiating joy and energy. My husband, though, stepped into her room and had to actually hold on to something to steady himself. "It looks like Kermit the Frog swallowed a hand grenade in here!" he exclaimed.

I grinned somewhat sheepishly, as I was having difficulty reconciling my absolute love for the room's color with my complete befuddlement of anyone who didn't see its sheer greatness. "Who knew you hated green?" I feebly croaked out (perhaps, pun intended).

The same "setting yourself up for success" concept of Rebbetzin Spetner that we mentioned previously can really be applied to the physical surroundings of our homes as well. We can set ourselves up for success with happiness by making our home places of visual joy. Even the Talmud in *Berachos* (57b) extols the virtues of having a beautiful home when it lists that two of the three things that bring a person comfort are a beautiful home and beautiful serving pieces or vessels.

There is a very informative book on setting ourselves up for success with our physical surroundings called *Joyful* by Ingrid Fetell Lee. Fetell Lee was an interior designer who did research on the visuals in our physical environments that make people happy. Eventually, with enough research, categories emerged that cut across lines of age, gender, and ethnicity that were found to be universally joyful for nearly everyone. Fetell Lee writes:

> *One day as I was studying the images, something clicked. I saw lollipops, pom poms, and polka dots, and it dawned on me: They were all round in shape. Vibrant quilts kept company with Matisse paintings and rainbow candies: all bursting with saturated color. A picture of a cathedral's rose window puzzled me at first, but when I placed it next to a snowflake and a sunflower, it made sense: all had radiating symmetries. And the common thread among bubbles, balloons and hummingbirds also became clear: They were all things that floated gently in the air...*

In all, she identified ten "aesthetics of joy," each of which reveals a distinct connection between the feeling of joy and the tangible qualities of the world around us:

Energy: vibrant color and light
Abundance: lushness, multiplicity, and variety
Freedom: nature, wildness, and open space
Harmony: balance, symmetry, and flow
Play: circles, spheres, and bubbly forms
Surprise: contrast and whimsy
Transcendence: elevation and lightness
Magic: invisible forces and illusions
Celebration: synchrony, sparkly and bursting shapes
Renewal: blooming, expansion, and curves

Many of these are easy to incorporate into our homes: a bold paint color, adding flowers (even fake ones) around our homes, or taking the time to plant some perennials in our gardens. Nowadays there are even beautiful wall decals that display giant vistas from all over the world and cost mere dollars, compared to in the past when owning something of similar beauty would have required investing in a costly piece of artwork.

My three-year-old son used to want to look for the moon every night, which of course is not the most convenient addition to a bedtime routine. This is especially true in a climate where the moon is often hidden behind clouds or just simply not visible from our skylight, and involves bundling up and going outside (not happening in Chicago winters). I finally solved the problem by bringing the moon to him—in his very room no less—with a floor-to-ceiling decal of the night sky with a full moon hanging over the ocean. Now all he needs is to point to it at bedtime, and boom, we have fulfilled our obligation of finding of the moon.

After the wild success of providing my son his own personal moon landing, I decided to try the same concept out for myself. Personally, I am very drawn to water, and since we live near Lake Michigan, I find it calling to me quite often. Each time I go, I leave with a sense of calm, awe, and wonder that lasts through much of my day thereafter. The only question is, how often can I really traipse over to the lake to refill my sense of wonder (especially during those cold Chicago months I mentioned)? And so, I decided that decals it is! Scattered strategically throughout the house, we now have giant decals of a tidal wave at sunset, a waterfall, and an image of an open window looking upon ocean waves (this last one is placed in a windowless basement room so it is especially helpful in negating the dungeon-doom feel).

When I feel I need a sense of awe or calm, I park myself in front of one of them and really stare at them, trying to feel as if I am there. Before you close this book and call me loony, know this: Research shows that our brains can't perceive a difference between real and imagined relaxation. This means that we can truly enjoy a restorative beach moment even in the middle of the winter, amid a pile of our kid's tossed boots and snow pants, while the heating system blazes at us from a vent. Try it. Most of the wall decals I found cost less than twenty dollars.

In another instance, God brought the visual comfort to me right when I needed it. There is a store called Home Goods that I love. One time, I found a beautiful fake floral arrangement and purchased it to place in our bedroom. Every morning, the giant pink flowers brought me so much joy that I snuck back to Home Goods several times to see if I could purchase another arrangement for my kitchen. The store didn't have it again until about a year later when the following story played out: One morning, as I was on pins and needles about certain news that was bound to come any day, I popped into Home Goods with only twenty minutes to spare between meetings and I finally found the exact type of floral arrangement I had been searching for all year. I happily bought it and triumphantly placed it in my kitchen. The very next day I got the news I had been waiting for, and it turned out to be bad. For that ensuing week, very few things brought me happiness. And yet, whenever I stepped into my kitchen and saw the gorgeous flower arrangement, something warm momentarily sparked in my heart. The feeling felt quite close to joy, almost like a reminder-jolt of the good in the world. One evening when I walked into the kitchen to serve my children dinner and felt that momentary zing out of my doldrums, the realization hit me.

"Hashem sent me flowers!" I called out to my kids, who glanced at each other like I had officially lost my mind. "He knew that I was going to get difficult news this week and so He made sure to put these in Home Goods and bring me there with just enough time to go to the aisle and find them," I explained. "I'm serious, *Chazal* tell us Hashem always brings the *refuah* (remedy) before the *makkah* (pain), and Hashem sent me these flowers to console me. He even placed them in the front of the store where they normally aren't displayed. Thank you, Hashem, for sending me flowers!"

We all had a good chuckle and long moment of enjoying the now-multidimensional beauty of those flowers. Thinking back, there are so many times God has sent me something to cheer me up in my life, be it a person with an uplifting message, a loving interaction, a well-timed success, or yes, even a physical item. It was just that I needed to take the time to notice those gifts.

There is so much we can't control in our homes: the sibling rivalry, children being prone to tantrums, or other behavioral nightmares that create impediments to *menuchas hanefesh* and joy. But we can certainly control what's on our walls. Don't be afraid of something new and different and try setting up your home environment for visual joy. Fetell Lee warns us humorously to not have "chromophobia," or in other words, fear of color. "The liveliness of color helps us marshal the energy we need to learn, be productive and grow," she writes. And so, at the end of the day, with the kids screaming in the background and the shoes and backpacks creating an obstacle course in your hall worthy of an Olympian, what's a little splattered Kermit the Frog between frazzled friends?

Where to Begin: Takeaways and Tips

🗩 Discussion Starters

- Talk to your children about what they love to look at the most. One of my children loves nature and animals, one loves bright colors, one loves when I put funny messages on the walls. Try to incorporate those things in their rooms.

⮕ Ready for Action

- Try to add one visual enhancement into each room of your house: Some suggestions are fake flowers and wall decals for joy, and pictures of *rabbanim* or Jerusalem for inspiration.
- Make some bright projects with your children and hang them up around your house in places that need more color. You could do a sticker mosaic or get some cheap canvases at the local craft store and download some of those step-by-step painting guides (there are many online) to make some realistic looking art.

CHAPTER 25

Circuit 20:
A Break from the
Great Indoors

*"Know the great reality, the richness of existence
that you always encounter. Contemplate its
grandeur, its beauty, its precision, its harmony."*

Rabbi Avraham Yitzchak Kook

"Trade screen time for green time."

Tagline for technology unplugging

There are many documented health and happiness benefits of being in the great outdoors: Getting sunlight in the morning has actually
been shown improve sleep better at night, which we know has been
linked to better moods and happiness (as we discussed at length in a
previous circuit). The microorganisms that get in the air along a dirt
path walk in the woods have been linked to better gut health. It has
been shown that hospital patients who can see trees from their room
windows recover more quickly.[1] And in Japan, the practice of what they
call "forest bathing" is proven to lower heart rate and blood pressure,

---

1   *Broken Brain 2*, docuseries by Dr. Mark Hyman.

reduce stress hormone production, boost the immune system, and improve overall feelings of well-being.[2]

This practice of immersing yourself in the woods became part of a national public health program in Japan in 1982 and over the years, Japanese officials have spent millions of dollars studying the physiological and psychological effects of "forest bathing." There are now forty-eight designated therapy trails in Japan based on the results of the research. Qing Li, a professor at Nippon Medical School in Tokyo, measured the activity of human natural killer (NK) cells in the immune system before and after exposure to the woods. In a 2009 study, Li's subjects showed significant increases in NK cell activity in the week after a forest visit, and positive effects lasted a month following each weekend in the woods. These cells are associated with immune system health and cancer prevention.

Nature is actually being prescribed to improve people's health and happiness. The only problem is that we are retreating back to our air-conditioning and blackout shades instead of filling the prescription, and our children are left peeking out from the window treatments longingly. An article by Louis Jack stated that today's kids spend less time outside than prison inmates:[3] The average child plays outside for just four to seven minutes daily. According to a study sponsored by the Environmental Protection Agency, the average American spends ninety percent of their time indoors and other sources say that by 2050, sixty-six of the world's population is projected to live in cities.

Several Torah authorities over the years have touted the importance of time outside as well. Rabbi Shlomo Wolbe advised young men to have an hour-long walk outside once a week,[4] and the following famous story of Rabbi Shimshon Raphael Hirsch emphasizes the importance of experiencing God's beautiful world: When asked why he was taking time away from learning to go see the Swiss Alps, Rabbi Hirsch responded, "I may have only a few years left, and when I stand before the Almighty on

---

2   https://time.com/5259602/japanese-forest-bathing/.
3   https://bit.ly/33rfUuf; https://natureplaysa.org.au/.
4   Mentioned in his *talmid*'s *sefer*, *Avnei Shlomo*, by Rabbi Yisrael Homnick.

Judgment Day, I don't want Him to ask me, 'Shimshon, why didn't you see My Alps?'" Appreciating the beauty of nature is built into our *mesorah* (tradition) as well; we have *berachos* that are to be said on several natural wonders such as the ocean, a rainbow, or even—as I learned on a recent trip—the Grand Canyon.

According to *The Washington Post*, there are several benefits of spending time outside that are significant for children specifically:[5]

1. **Better school performance**: Time spent in nature and increased fitness improve cognitive function.

2. **More creativity**: Outdoor play uses and nurtures the imagination.

3. **Much higher levels of fitness**: Children are more active when they are outdoors.

4. **More friends**: Children who organize their own games and participate in unstructured group activities are less solitary and learn to interact with their peers.

5. **Less depression and hyperactivity**: Time in nature is soothing, improves mood, and reduces stress. For kids who spend more time on screens, outdoor time has also been found to increase attention spans, because things in nature move at a slower pace than they generally do on screens.

6. **Stronger bones**: Exposure to natural light helps prevent vitamin D deficiency, making outdoorsy children less vulnerable to bone problems, cardiovascular disease, diabetes, and other health issues.

7. **Improved eyesight**: More children are developing nearsightedness because of the time that they spend looking at close screens such as on tablets, and therefore time spent outdoors can help mitigate this.

8. **Better sleep**: Exposure to natural light and lots of physical activity help reset a child's natural sleep rhythm.

---

5   Taken from https://wapo.st/3idXKC1.

Getting outdoors has also been shown to increase the parts of the brain linked to empathy, love, and emotional stability. A study by the University of Chicago found that people in neighborhoods with green space and trees reported a better ability to cope with life's demands and stresses. The University of Minnesota reported that time spent outside impacts the endocrine, immune, and nervous system.

Convinced yet?

It can be hard to supervise our children while they are outside, and with growing dangers in the world, watching over them feels more and more necessary. However, the good news is that there are nonetheless many ways to work more outdoor time into our children's lives. One of my mentors solved this problem by fencing in her backyard completely with locks on the fence gates. In this way, she was thrilled to be able to consider the backyard as just another room of her house. The cost of the gates was justified by the advantage of being able to use the backyard as a "giant family room," and she would bundle her kids up to spend time in "that part of the house" no matter what the season. In the winter they played in the snow, in the fall they raked leaves and jumped into piles, and during the summer they had water fights while she cooked in the kitchen and watched them through a window. Fencing it in gave *her* the peace of mind to send out those of her children old enough to be out there without constant supervision, and gave *her children* the peace of getting time in nature.

Another tip is to build in a ten-minute park stop on your way home as part of a routine. It could be on the way back from school, errands, or anything in-between. Putting it in the schedule ensures it will happen, even if you don't have a backyard to fence in. Another great tip is to garden more. Whether your link to the outdoors is an apartment windowsill or an entire yard of possibilities, you can plant easy herbs or even small vegetable plants that children love tending to. Our favorites are cherry tomato plants and cilantro. I've written multiple stories, including one published in *Chicken Soup for the Gardener's Soul*, about the memories I have of gardening as a child. One treasured adventure included a watermelon plant and neighboring zucchini plant that swapped identities: A puny watermelon was somehow produced alongside zucchini-zilla! I still remember spending a whole afternoon with my mother, cooking as many zucchini dishes as we could think of, all from that same monster zucchini.

Taking small actions can create big nature opportunities for our children and even outdoor creatures. Planting native plants can transform any space into a bustling wildlife destination and help children cultivate a love of nature. We are not talking about a skunk garden here, but something more like milkweed to attract monarch butterflies!

Personally, I also find it a worthwhile investment to buy outdoor toys and activities. A bucket of chalk costs way less than a half hour with a babysitter, and often entertains children much longer. Not to mention, any adventure in art that has a locked door separating between the project and my light gray carpet gets a green light in my book. Give children a purpose for their chalk art. For example, sometimes I'll hand them a new bucket before Purim and tell them to make a giant welcome path for the costumed merrymakers dropping off *mishloach manos*, before Sukkos we can have another welcome path leading the way to the sukkah, and before guests with children come to stay over, we've made other forms of welcome signs and games (chalk hopscotch, an obstacle course, etc.). We have experienced a few weather debacles when I didn't quite pay attention to the forecast before commissioning these works of art. So please learn from my mistakes and make sure you don't have the art formed before a rainstorm or you'll end up with a bunch of pouty Picassos.

Another thing we love is relay races. Give your children a few plastic spoons and a bag of beans and suddenly they have an hour-long adventure in seeing who can carry the most beans without dropping them from the spoon to various areas of the yard. There are many relay-race variations; often, once you give your children a few ideas they get creative on their own and take it from there.

Whatever it takes, get your children out of your hair and into nature's embrace. You might even find yourself following them outside and enjoying the health benefits and childlike fun as well. I recently dominated at four-square, jumped rope, and even learned to ride a hoverboard, all under the guise of "supervision duties."

Where to Begin: Takeaways and Tips

➔ Ready for Action

- Challenge yourself to get your children out into nature for at least fifteen minutes a day over the next two weeks.
- Pick some new activities from the chapter to do with your children outside the next time they say they are bored inside.
- Visit a new park you've never been to as a family (we found an amazing one several neighborhoods away with two-story slides and a splash pad area).
- Take a family Shabbos walk.
- Plan a family nature outing on a Sunday when you would normally have chosen an indoor activity: Bring a bag for each child to fill with collected nature items and then have them glue each on a poster board or paper at home to make an art project (such as creating a "name sign" that they can then hang out their bedroom doors). Alternatively, have each family member create a story out of the items in their bag, either telling the tale using the items as props or parts of the plot.
- Plan a family bike ride. There likely are beautiful trails to discover right in your area. For example, just in the past few years I discovered a path near my house that goes all the way to the Chicago Botanic Gardens and another along the famous Chicago Lake Shore Drive that goes all the way downtown. There is now even a bike path that goes across the entire United States![6]

✂ Tools

- Invest in outdoor toys: chalk, bouncy balls, sandbox, croquet set, cornhole board, badminton set (all personal family favorites).

---

6   https://discoverytrail.org/.

- Consider investing in fencing with locking gates to make the yard like any other "room" of your house.
- Put a reminder notification in your calendar to regularly stop at a park on your way home from school or at another part of your day.

Light at the Middle of the Tunnel

Finding Your Own Happiness as a Parent

CHAPTER 26

Circuit 21:
Self-Care

"If I am not for me, who is for me?...And if not now, when?"

Hillel, Pirkei Avos 1:14

"You need to put on your own oxygen mask first before your child's."

Airline Safety Presentation

Modeling is the greatest teaching method in parenting; it is our most potent tool. We addressed this in depth in circuit 17, "Displaying Joy Yourself," where we talked about the approach of "fake it until you make it" happiness. Still, a parenting book on teaching children happiness would be incomplete without a section on helping parents find *real* happiness themselves. There is a saying that I have heard men say: "Happy wife, happy life." But as we noted earlier, the same is true for our children: "Happy parents, happy kids." Now it's time to take our exploration to the next level and to guide you with some steps toward the real thing for yourself.

So how do we do this? "Self-care" has certainly become a hot topic in our times, but I believe that this concept is often understood the wrong way. Self-care only goes as far as its goal: if its aim is to help create space and bolster a life in which we are happy, outside of dedicated self-care mode, then that's great. But if self-care is used just as an escape from a life we are unhappy with, then it will only get you that far—as an escape—which by definition will put us right back in an unchanged reality we are unhappy with once self-care time is over.

In the words of writer Brianna Wiest:

> *True self-care is not salt-baths and chocolate cake; it is making the choice to build a life you don't need to regularly escape from...A world in which self-care has to be such a trendy topic is a world that is sick. Self-care should not be something we resort to because we are so absolutely exhausted that we need some reprieve from our own relentless internal pressure...It is not satiating your immediate desires. It is letting go. It is choosing new...it is letting yourself be normal. Regular. Unexceptional. It is sometimes having a dirty kitchen and deciding that your ultimate goal isn't going to be having abs...If you find yourself having to regularly indulge in consumer self-care it's because you are disconnected from actual self-care which has very little to do with "treating yourself" and a whole lot to do with parenting yourself and making choices for your long-term wellness.*[1]

This is good news for those who can't afford or justify a luxury vacation or professional massage at regular intervals, but it is also good news for those who can—and yet still feel empty and stressed within hours after the return home to the chaos of everyday life.

In order to get to the heart of true self-care and healing, we have to deal with what is really bothering us. We need to go deep and not distract ourselves from these problems but fix and heal them. Along with learning new approaches, one of the best things we can do is unlearn old ones; get rid of the dead weight of habits and automatic responses that simply do not serve us well. In the words of Burnett and Evans in their book *Designing Your Life*, "Unlearning things is often harder and more important than learning things."

---

1   https://bit.ly/35iuUNh.

Either way, the crux of the matter is that there is so much we can do to learn, unlearn, and rebuild, and many ways to give ourselves true self-care in the process:

- For some, it could mean therapy.
- For some, it could mean meditation or mindfulness.
- For some, it could mean making the time to daven or learn more.
- For some, it could mean getting rid of toxic relationships.
- For some, it could mean more quality time with friends or family.
- For some, it could mean making time to do more *chessed*.
- And for some, it could genuinely mean a bubble bath.

But back to the words of Wiest, truly effective self-care has a targeted definition:

> *It means being the hero of your life, not the victim. It means re-writing what you have until your everyday life isn't something you need therapy to recover from. It is no longer choosing a life that looks good over a life that feels good…It means meeting your own needs so you aren't anxious or dependent on other people (or their constant approval)…It is becoming the kind of person you know you want to be and are meant to be. Someone who knows that salt baths and chocolate cake are ways to enjoy life—not to escape from it.*

Practice this type of self-care and work the skills of the section 2 circuits into your own life as well. Plants only bask in the glow of sunshine; they can't just be told to produce it themselves. If our children see that we are using the tools that we have talked about in the circuits, they are more likely to as well. Talk to them about your own struggles with happiness and about how you ultimately found it, and they will know it is OK to struggle too. Be open, be honest, and show a growth mindset toward happiness and life in general.

And now, I present some certified self-care options, none of which should take more than five to thirty minutes of your day. Choose from the list based on what you need the most on any particular day (quiet time, social interaction, emotional boost). Depending on how much time you have to dedicate to your happiness muscles, pick something each day that you can incorporate into your routine. Please make yourself and your happiness a priority. It will trickle down to your progeny. And they *are* watching!

CHAPTER 27

Circuit 22:
Shedding Some Light on
Your Own Happiness

Mix-and-Match Happiness Menu

- Go for a walk or make a coffee-date with a friend. At least for women, research shows that getting together with a close friend at least twice a week increases overall happiness.
- Nataly Kogan, author of *Happier Now*, recommends a five-minute "joy break." This is kind of like a coffee break, but one where you immerse yourself in a happy thought, fresh air, good music (or I would add, Torah), for five full minutes. Pick whatever it is that gives you a boost of happiness and peace. This could also be something different every day.
- Five minutes of hard-core exercise (running in place, stair climbing, jumping jacks) to get your body's endorphins going. These hormones give you a physiological boost of good feelings.
- Unburden yourself: pick something you have been putting off and just go ahead and get it over with today. Make that difficult phone call, pay that bill, make the decision, confront that person, or run to that store. Unburden your mind with the relief that the task has been done.
- At the end of your day, write down the small moments that brought you joy (a compliment from your child, a hug, sunlight that streamed into your window that morning, a quiet moment

in carpool line, a call from a friend, a stranger handing you a coupon). After you write them down, review the list and as Nataly Kogan would say, "swim in the joy of these little moments."

- At the end of your day, write down any Divine Providence moments from that day (an elevated gratitude journal, so to speak). If you train yourself to notice them, you'll notice that every day has some. It could be your children falling off of something and not getting hurt (I have witnessed several tumbles that were nothing less than a miracle when my children came out unscathed). Perhaps you were running late to an appointment and then all the traffic lights you encountered were green and you got there on time. Maybe the power went out, but you were able to save all the perishable fridge items and bring them to a friend who still had power (and room in her fridge/freezer!) before anything spoiled. It could be that your baby slept through the night when you really needed it. And of course, there are the big things too (having a healthy baby, getting that raise you needed at work, or even things that you thought you wanted but didn't get and yet it worked out for the best).

- Do the following body scan: Sit quietly and just notice and enjoy the miracle that is your body—how your heart beats, the rise and fall of your chest as you breathe, which parts of your body feel heavy and which parts feel light, what you perceive in that moment around you via each of your five senses (what sounds, sights, smells, tastes, and touches your senses are picking up).

- Try something new, and spend a few minutes getting better at it every day. Watch a video about how to do it, go to your craft store and get supplies, take out a how-to book or just ask a friend to teach you. According to Albert Einstein, "If a person studies a subject for fifteen minutes a day, in a year he will be an expert. In five years, he will be a national expert."

Pick a Mindfulness Activity

Here are some suggestions:

- Pick a noise trigger for today—your incoming text message beep, your children calling out "Mommy," or perhaps every time you hear the neighbor's dog bark. Every time you hear that noise for the rest of today, take a full deep breath (in through your nose and out from your mouth) before you do anything else. That's all it takes to turn an ordinary occurrence into a chance to do something relaxing for yourself.

- Take a paper and write down five things that brighten your day *as you come across them*. This is different than the exercise above because you write them down in the moment. It could be your child putting their head in your lap, the smell of the fresh cut grass that your gardener cut, or the fact that you had enough leftovers from the night before to save you from cooking dinner tonight.

- Try mindful eating. When you eat a meal or snack today, don't wolf through it while distracted. Instead, focus completely on the food: its taste, its color, its smell, its temperature, its texture. You'll notice how much more you enjoy the meal and feel satisfied by it.

- Sit still and revel in a great memory for five minutes. Remember as many details as you can and recreate how you felt during that memory. It will help escape the "negativity bias" that our brains cling to.

- Try practicing mindfulness during a chore today. Focus on the warm bubbles and sound of the water as you wash dishes; listen to the swish of the broom and enjoy the beauty of neat piles after you sweep; do slow, relaxing breathing as you clear off the breakfast dishes. It'll make you feel like you maximized your chore time by elevating it to relaxation time.

- Take a break from your phone during one task today: for example, during a drive, a walk to the bus stop to get your children, or on an errand. Notice whether unplugging makes you feel more plugged in to the things that matter most.

- Give yourself positive feedback. Take a few minutes to be kind to yourself and reflect on what areas you are excelling in, and what areas of difficulty you are improving on.
- Take a "noticing walk" where you aim to see things you didn't notice before in your area. The goal is to get you out of your head and into your surroundings.
- Lie on the floor for a few minutes. This actually helps stretch out your back, lengthens the spine, and creates more space in the belly for breathing. It also gives you a quick rest.
- Use your car time at red stoplights today to take full, deep breaths. See how this makes each stoplight a delightful pause instead of an inconvenience.
- Give yourself a foot massage. There is a whole field of reflexology that is built on the idea that the nerves in the feet are a map of the whole body. Therefore, pampering your feet can relax and rejuvenate many more parts of you.
- Close your eyes and gently press your palms over your eyelids, massaging very gently. "Go dark" like this for a couple of minutes to relax.

Several of these suggestions were adapted from Stress Less by Kate Hanley. Please see the book for more suggestions.

CHAPTER 28

Circuit 23:
The Power of Unplugging

"Shema Yisrael does not mean 'Hear, O Israel.' It means something like: Listen. Concentrate. Give the word of God your most focused attention. Strive to understand. Engage all your faculties, intellectual and emotional."

Rabbi Lord Jonathan Sacks

"Almost everything will work again if you unplug it for a few minutes, including you."

Anne Lamott

In Judaism, focus is of paramount importance: focus in davening, focus during mitzvah performance, and even focus in the teaching of our children. *Rashi* interprets "You shall *teach these things diligently* to your children" in *Kiddushin* (30a) as "You shall *sharpen* your children," meaning, teach them the full depth of understanding so they will be able to recall what they learn. This is difficult to do while distracted. One would never sharpen a knife while focusing elsewhere, for fear of physical danger. So too, with this important charge of sharpening our children, we should fear the spiritual danger of not passing along our *mesorah* with intention and focus.

Among the myriad distractions in our modern lives, I believe the biggest culprit is technology. I know by now we have all been warned about the many dangers of digital devices, especially their addictive nature. One thing we may not be realizing, though, is how much technology has fragmented our attention, making us deeply distracted even when we are not actively using it.

Just like in circuit 18 where we spoke about the importance of letting children be bored so their intelligence juices can flow and their thoughts can creatively wander, the same is true of our own adult minds. If we are afraid of being in the silence of our own thoughts for too long and feel the need to check our phones the moment they beep, we are losing an opportunity to be in our own brain long enough to let it be a unified whole. We turn ourselves into fragmented slaves to the distractions around us.

"Thoughts never stop. All you can do is stop interacting with them, stop listening to them," says Eline Snel, the mindfulness expert we quoted earlier in section 2. The same is true of technology. You cannot stop interacting with the flow of media as long as it's on, because it is always *flowing*. There is always a breaking news story, a new post on social media, a new direct message or email we could get lost in. Turn off the phone and we lose the physiological trigger of its ping (yes it has been shown, much like Pavlov and his dogs, that we react physiologically to even the ping of an incoming message).

What I am saying is that we need to "unplug" to turn on ourselves, to get off the autopilot of waiting to hear if someone else is contacting us, or if there is something to see that we are missing on that little rectangular device that can easily become our master. I can't tell you how many times I have witnessed, much to my dismay, the scenario in a restaurant where two or more people have clearly taken the time to go out to enjoy each other's company, and yet one or more of them is just sitting there on their phone. When did the person right in front of us become less important than a voice inside of a little box, being transmitted from hundreds or sometimes thousands of miles away?

Research backs up how unhappy this is making people. I have a friend who is a professor at an Israeli university that runs a program for *chareidi* women. This friend did research on the happiness levels of *chareidi* women Facebook users, versus *chareidi* women who do not use Facebook. She found, across the board, that the ones who used Facebook were less happy. She told me this was all the impetus she needed for getting off Facebook herself, and she reported being much happier after having done so.

Part of the thinking is that being in constant touch with other people who are trying to show the "best image of themselves" through pictures on WhatsApp, social media posts, and even text messages makes us compare ourselves to them. And usually, once we go into comparison-mode, we feel we are coming up short. In general, comparison usually leads us to unhappiness, and yet right now, we have a device in our possession that allows us to carry out social comparisons constantly with the push of a button or swipe of a finger. It's no wonder technology can make us miserable.

Even more so, our devices allow us to see what's going on anywhere in the world at any time. Considering that the media loves to highlight the horrible, it is understandable how being in touch with the whole universe is much more overwhelming than focusing on what's going on right in front of us at our kitchen table.

I can tell you that during the first several months of the Coronavirus pandemic, I only read limited news stories because I found them too overwhelming. I told my husband and other people in my life who were constantly updating me on the pandemic infection rate and death toll to put me on a "need to know" basis and to not discuss it with me unless absolutely necessary. I was already on lockdown in my house anyway, so I didn't see how it would help to constantly be bombarded by the "numbers" and horrific stories of death sweeping the world. My job was to stay inside (both literally and figuratively) and focus on what was in front of me in order to help my family get through it however possible.

Everyone can set their own boundaries, but its best that there be conscious boundaries. Maybe it's not owning a smartphone. Maybe if you do need to own a smartphone, it means taking social media apps off your phone. Maybe no phones in the kitchen during family dinner. Maybe the phone is turned off after 8:00 PM so we can focus on other things inside our own home and head. Maybe the phone has an "away" message during car rides so we are not tempted to rifle through our purses at stop lights, unable to just breathe in the peace of sitting there for the next thirty seconds.

Children notice our distractions. Before I set boundaries, my children would say things like, "There you are on your phone again" or "I wish you would pay as much attention to me as you do to your phone." I would feel angry and defensive, brushing the comments off as rude and untrue. It took a while to realize that there was nothing more exciting on my phone than the little faces in front of me, desperate for eye contact and undivided attention. Just physically sitting in the playroom with them while being on my phone wasn't enough, they could sense that my real presence wasn't there.

I now try to tell them out loud when I am putting my phone away, so they can appreciate that I am moving it aside and choosing them over my little distraction. I try to set times when I can check my texts, messages, and emails instead of being pulled by the ping. Even as I write this book, I find myself distracted by the urge to check my email, look at the news, see what people are talking about on WhatsApp. But when I resist the urge to look, I can feel my brain being put back together, I can feel my sense of focus reclaiming my own attention. I'm old enough that I lived in an age without these electronic necessities, when there wasn't anything else to do on a park bench than speak to other people around you and ahem, watch the kids (back then I was babysitting, but still). I remember speaking to strangers at the grocery store checkout lines to pass the time instead of forming a single file of zombies scrolling through their phones to make the wait tolerable. People were more connected back then, not only to each other but to themselves.

Let's reclaim what we can and be good role models for our children who will never know that bygone era. Let's show them that we have control over our technology and not the other way around.

CHAPTER 29

Circuit 24:
The Four Ps of Non-Frenetic Parenting

"There are no problems, only opportunities for growth."

Rebbetzin Dena Weinberg

"A mind is like a parachute; it does not work if it is not open."

Frank Zappa

Parenting is very demanding, and there is not much to do to slow down the roller coaster once it starts. There are a few things we can do, though, to have relaxing effects on this frenetic and sometimes frantic aspect of our lives. These things are: (1) patience, (2) presence, (3) pressure release, and (4) present moment acceptance. Let's look at them one by one.

Patience

Patience should be no shock. Turning balls of energy into refined human beings who channel that energy into productivity does not happen overnight. Nor does it happen over a few years either. When we give birth to a child, we are making a long-term investment that will take many years to generate "returns." This might very well be the area of our lives that will require the most patience.

Recently, one of my daughters broke her arm and had to have surgery to place pins in the bone while it healed. There were several experiences during those two days in the hospital that were excruciating for her, and I tried to break them into small pieces to manage the patience they required. For example, inserting the IV tube was difficult, so when the medical staff had to replace one and my daughter was freaking out, I drew close to her face, looked her in the eye and said, "A person can do almost anything for ten seconds. We are going to split this experience into ten-second pieces and get through them together, one manageable piece at a time." I held my fixed gaze on her brown eyes that mirrored my own and breathed in and out with her, counting ten seconds while they poked around her arm. When those ten seconds ended and they had still made no progress but caused significant pain, I repeated the same line and told her that we were going to bravely start again; it was now a new ten seconds, and a person can endure almost anything for ten seconds. We started the breathing again. Unfortunately, this went on several cycles while they ineptly dug around her arm, but at least by breaking it into manageable slices of time, I was able to help her get through it. I've applied this concept to my own parenting patience struggles as well.

Sometimes it involves listening to a tantrum, sometimes it involves rocking a child to sleep while I myself am exhausted and just want to get back into my bed. Sometimes it involves being at an insanely loud arcade or play space alone, juggling all my children in the chaos and desperately wanting to leave and go home, but knowing the kids are having fun and we have to stay. Usually, I have to slice it into ten-minute increments. When I am able to say, "A person can deal with almost anything for ten minutes," I empower myself by putting a timeline on the noise and the haste, and after that, I just break it up to another ten minutes if need be. This doesn't help on the macro level with the long timeline of almost two decades of parenting while our children live at home (after all, twenty years broken up into ten-minute increments is still daunting)! But as they say, the days are long and the years are short. Patience is what gets us through the days, and the inevitable momentum of time flying gets us through the years.

Presence

Presence means accepting being in the here and now, both the good and the bad. It's noticing the feeling of the small, buttery-soft, warm hand in yours. But it's also presence with the problems, like when your children come home crying because they were bullied at school. The more we allow ourselves to be present, the less we miss and feel guilty about later on. Be there for your children. Show up. That is half of parenting right there; it gives children the confidence that they can rely on people. You are their first test case of someone they can rely on, so be mindful of the fact that you are creating their prototype for trust.

Pressure Release

Pressure release means not pressuring yourself with notions of perfection. There is no perfect parenting, and our children will be fine with "good enough" parenting. Children are more resilient than we think. So make your best effort but let yourself be human as well. When we release the internal pressure, we form more realistic and attainable parenting goals.

Present Moment Acceptance

Present moment acceptance in parenting applies to both our children and ourselves, without excluding or rejecting any aspect of either. With us, this means forgiving ourselves when we yell at our children or do something that wasn't ideal modeling in the present moment, but still taking ownership, admitting what we did was wrong, and apologizing. With children this means, in the words of Eline Snel, "Acceptance of all those moments when they fail to meet your expectations, yell when they ought to be quiet, forget to thank Grandma for her lovely present, appear to be ungrateful, or assume you have extremely thick skin." In other words, try your best not to take these things personally, and you will relieve a tremendous amount of the internal pressure you feel as a parent.

Try to make those little balls of raw energy the best children they can be, try to always help them grow, but realize that much of parenting success is *siyata d'Shmaya* (Divine assistance). At the end of the day, children need to be true to themselves and know we will love them "בַּאֲשֶׁר הוּא שָׁם," in the process of becoming the masterpieces they, God willing, will ultimately be.

CHAPTER 30

Circuit 25:
Parents as Team Players

"If you have a fault, be the first to say it."

Talmud, Bava Kama 92b

"United we stand, divided we fall."

Aesop

Ever heard of Winchester, Virginia? It was the center of one of the most fascinating fights during the American Civil War. The city changed hands a remarkable seventy-four times, being handed back and forth between the northern and southern states over and over again, as the two sides returned repeatedly to fighting about its ownership.

We all have our own Winchester, Virginias in our marriages—those pesky issues that never seem to get resolved and yet we fall into the familiar patterns of fighting over them whenever they rear their heads. According to Dr. John Gottman, expert in the field of marriage and family therapy, sixty-nine percent of marriage conflicts are never resolved.

In general, any disagreements can bring strain on a marriage, but one of the most destructive points of tension are when those fights revolve around different approaches to raising children. These fights can center around *chinuch* (education), approaches to punishment, dealing with a difficult child, or even the medical care of a chronically ill child. Many a marriage has dissolved over fighting often about the offspring.

It is a natural topic about which tensions can run high—both parties are highly invested, not just because of love but also because of legacy. I'm sure that we have all heard the importance of "parenting as a unit" or "showing a united front to the children," but how do we achieve this practically when the stakes are so high and we disagree?

It is beyond the scope of this book to go into the nitty-gritty of marriage advice, but what I would like to bring out in this chapter is that the more we can come to a meeting of the minds on our parenting approaches behind closed doors, the better it will be for our own happiness, and by extension, the happiness of our children. Parenting as partners should be the ultimate goal in the home.

Working on this can take many forms. A common approach is to fight better to fight less. In other words, try not to let yourself get sucked into the same loop of "he said, she said." Instead, turn it more into a discussion, with both of you reminding each other that you are open to collaboration. Sometimes, just hearing the other side say these words can be reassuring, because often, when a fight begins, both sides retreat into competition mode, forgetting they are on the same team and looking to collaborate. Once you are in discussion mode, leave time for each side to think about what the other side said before coming to a conclusion and making the decision. After all, if it's an issue you are fighting about all the time anyway, it's probably worth it to let it simmer overnight while everyone reflects on the talking points of the other side.

It also takes the tension out of decisions when we frame them as temporary: "Let's try this for a week/month/year and then we can re-evaluate." That way, when you give in to the other side, you don't have to feel "locked" into an approach.

Here are some good general tips that I've modified from the Center for Parenting Education on effective team parenting:

- Set aside a regular time to discuss issues that have been coming up with the children and plan strategies for the upcoming week.
- If one of you wants to try a new approach, ask your spouse for support or, at a minimum, non-interference.
- Avoid evading responsibility when a problem arises. Deal with issues as they occur.
- Don't interfere with a situation the other person is handling.
- After problems have been solved, allow time to talk about the interactions and to give suggestions, praise, support, or constructive criticism for how they were handled.
- Resolve differences of opinion in private, not in front of your children.
- Don't let your children play one of you off of the other. If you say no to something and then your children go ask the other parent looking for a yes, don't let that second decision stand.

Some other modified suggestions from the Center for Parenting Education on how to handle disagreements as they come up are:

- **Stick to the issue at hand**: Try your best not to go on tangents, revisit old issues, or bring up other complaints. Stay in the now and discuss one issue at a time.
- **Use first-person "I" statements**: This is a way to communicate your thoughts and feelings without blaming or attacking the other person. This skill involves remaining calm and clear, or in other words, assertive but not aggressive. For example, "I am concerned that your punishment was more severe than it had to be."

- **Accept that you and your partner may have different perspectives**: Don't take it as a personal affront that your spouse disagrees with you. There may be more than one valid perspective on an issue. The goal is to come together and decide how you want to lead your family.
- **Focus on solutions**: Don't get involved in the blame game. If a problem arises with a child's behavior, the question that needs to be addressed is how to handle it and not whose fault it is.
- **Avoid lecturing**: To decrease defensiveness, stay calm and communicate your reactions in a non-generalizing way. Avoid saying things like "You always do this," or "I can never count on you."
- **Talk with your spouse directly**: Don't shut each other out and begin communicating through your children. It is awkward and often inappropriate for a child to be used as a middleman. Model direct communication and compromise. It will also help reduce opportunities for your children to manipulate you by playing one of you against the other.[1]

The bottom line is, when we fight about our children, everyone in the household suffers. Try to be as unified as possible; if all else fails with compromise, try taking turns making decisions as you work out unifying your approach.

And lastly, know that everyone has their Winchester, Virginias. Just try not to change your decisions on those issues seventy-four times.

---

1   https://parenting-ed.org/for-parents/.

CHAPTER 31

Circuit 26:
Adult Friendships

"Two are better than one...for if they fall, one will lift up his fellow."

Mishlei 4:9–10

"Sometimes your circle decreases in size but increases in value."

Anonymous

Let's be honest, friendships in adulthood are slow-growing. As we leave our school years, we are suddenly thrust out of our "friendship incubator," where we spent every single weekday with the exact same people in the exact same building or campus, talking, laughing, and processing every millisecond of our lives. It was only natural that we would end up liking one or two or thirty people there…

Then, when we leave our school years and perhaps even move to a new community, we are thrown into the working, learning, or stay-at-home-parenting world. Suddenly, the only time we have to bond with the strangers around us is twenty minutes a week during *kiddush* after shul, Shabbos meals where we attempt to have a cohesive conversation in thirty-parts-or-more while being interrupted by our children, or by going out of our way to make plans with these strangers outside of the demands of everyday life. Then, many times we end up moving to a new

179

place and having to start all over again (my husband and I did this seven times in the first seven years of our marriage). Needless to say, it's a less than perfect recipe for long-term-friendship success...rinse and repeat.

There came a time that I all but gave up. After moving so many times I began to call the friendships that I made in each of our brief sojourns, "single-serve friendships" because I knew they were bound to run out once we moved in a year or so. By the fifth location I was deflated and barely made any effort. I said to myself, "Better to just invest my time in my oldie-but-goodie friendships over the phone." After all, nothing is quite like the friendship of someone who's known you forever, correct?

The answer I found to this reflection is...no and yes. No, there is nothing quite like an old friend, but yes, we do need to make the effort to invest in new friendships in our adulthood as well, especially if we are far away from our old friends. Yes, adult friendships are slow-growing, given the limited time that most of us have to develop them, but once they sprout, they can be just as beautiful as old ones. *Tiferes Yisrael* on *Pirkei Avos* (4:14) adds that a lot of growth happens when you move to a place where people didn't know you as a child; you can actually develop your persona further when you are no longer stuck with oudated labels.

For the first four years I lived in Chicago, I felt very alone. My husband had two very demanding jobs that caused him to be working seven days a week (don't worry, the one on Shabbos was as a shul *rav*), and I was at home all day taking care of the children. Most of my close childhood friends were in different time zones and busy with their own adventures, and we were lucky if we caught time to chat more than once a month. I only made one new true-blue close friend in my city during those first years and I tried to focus on the old saying, "All you need is one real friend." Except, the saying never covered what to do if that friend moved to Florida...

After that, I knew I had to be more proactive in carving out time to develop new friendships. I found a gorgeous path near Lake Michigan and began to invite other mothers to bundle up their children and join me there for walks. The excitement in the responses I got was encouraging. Not only were most of these other handpicked new "friendship candidates" looking to bond and develop new friendships too, but the thought of getting some exercise out on a beautiful walking path thrilled them as well. I had some epic talks on those walks and many friendships were formed while the children happily took in the majestic beach view and ate snacks in their strollers. When they got restless, we would stop at a park and keep talking. I found this to be way more conducive to real conversation than when I would go on mommy-and-me playdates to people's houses and we could barely hear each other over the din of children occasionally playing, but mostly needing our attention.

These new friendships have become my mainstays. Many of our children are now all school age and we continue to walk together on that same beach path, supporting each other through life's up and downs and having a good laugh at the humor we find in them. I try to make time for coffee with friends and the occasional Shabbos walk as well, realizing now how important those friendships are in developing and maintaining who I am as an individual outside of family life. We mutually benefit from the IV drip of support these friendships provide when we need a listening ear or have the opportunity to be the lending ear.

Don't underestimate the happiness and *menuchas hanefesh* value of new friendships or maintaining close ties with old ones in adulthood. Even with the limited time we have in a given day, these are worth the investment. Which brings me to Tool 1...

SECTION FOUR

Forming Your Tool Kit

CHAPTER 32

Tool 1:
Finding Your Village

How to Filter Advice
and Find the People to Advise You

"A person should always attach himself to good people."

Talmud, Bava Basra 109b

"It takes a village to raise a child."

African Proverb

There is a famous African proverb that says, "It takes a village to raise a child." This applies very strongly to the Jewish community as well. There are many people who help a child become their best self. These include, *morahs*, *rabbeim*, the shul *rav* and *rebbetzin*, peer group, extended family, professionals, community members, and more. So many people are influencing our children and modeling behavior for them.

But what is unique about our community is that the village that helps children grow doesn't only influence the children, but it affects the parents as well. Because Judaism puts such an emphasis on personal and lifelong growth, as adults, we too are always growing and looking to refine ourselves. The parenting realm is no different. Just think about how many speakers come to your community every year to speak about parenting. Now think about how many conversations you have with your friends and peers about parenting. There are so many different approaches, a person's head could spin. So how do we filter through advice and influences? How do we know what approach is personally right for us and our children? And most importantly, how do we "handpick" our village?

I led a bi-monthly *vaad*/personal growth group for young married ladies, and the topic of influences came up. One woman told over the scenario of a friend who loves having Shabbos guests. This friend invites a lot of people weekly but then finds herself becoming quickly overwhelmed with the preparations on Fridays and ends up putting her children in front of a screen all afternoon while she cooks and cleans. The woman who mentioned this story was upset because she felt her friend was making the wrong trade-off by picking Shabbos guests over taking care of her children. However, she was even more upset because now there was a little voice in her head that piped up with a suggestion on Erev Shabbos as the preparations loomed and her young son was screaming. "Maybe a few minutes with a screen wouldn't hurt?" it whispered.

Another *vaad* attendee disagreed with the black-and-white notion of judging this situation at face value. She postured that maybe the particular mitzvah of *hachnasas orchim* (welcoming guests) gave this woman a lot of *chizuk* and joy over Shabbos, and so as long as she was an attentive mother the rest of the time, what did one afternoon matter? A heated debate raged on, but the central question that emerged was: "If you are in a friend's home and they do something that doesn't resonate with you (using more screen time than you allow, yelling at their children, etc.), is this the right person to be friends with, and if so, how do you prevent those things from affecting or subtly influencing you?"

It was at this point that I brought in the *Rambam*'s famous piece on *Pirkei Avos* 1:6, where he discusses friendships. The *Rambam* classifies three types of friends: a friend for benefit, a friend for enjoyment, and a friend for virtue:

- A friend for **benefit** is someone you spend time with because there is some other benefit other than friendship involved. For example, your children are friends, so you all get together for playdates, or you live on the same block and chat outside while waiting for the school bus. This is a friendship of convenience.

- A friend for **enjoyment** is the next level and is further split by the *Rambam* into two types: the friend for pleasure and the friend for confidence. The friendship for pleasure is when you like doing similar activities and so you seek each other out to enjoy them together. For example, you are both in knitting group, book club, or attend the same weekly *shiur*. The other type is the friend for confidence, who you enjoy on an emotional level. This is a friend you can really speak to, either to unburden your heart or to enjoy a conversation about life with. This is a friend you can be yourself around without fearing any loss from speaking freely. You know that your words will be kept in confidence.
- Lastly, there is a friend for **virtue**, a friendship where the two of you are striving for some greater good together and you make each other better people through the process. The *Rambam* says about this type, "Each one wants to be helped by his friend in reaching this good for both of them together. And this is the friend which He commanded to acquire."

What I then suggested to my *vaad* is that sometimes it is helpful to mentally classify and know which friend fits into which of the *Rambam*'s categories and by doing so, we then understand what role they fit in our lives. For example, if we recognize that some friends are really a "friend for convenience or benefit," then when we see them doing things we don't agree with or they give us advice that doesn't resonate with us, it won't sink in very deeply. However, when someone we deem as a friend for virtue gives us advice, we will think it over more and really take it to heart. In addition, knowing this classification helps us seek out more friends for virtue, people we know will elevate us.

The hope is that we will not fall into the complacency of just accepting all our "friendships of convenience" as the best friendships we can make in adulthood, thereby being OK with mediocre influences. It's easy to find someone to have fun with, and much harder to find someone you can grow with. But once you do, hold on to them tight and truly be an integral part of each other's villages. The payoffs are immeasurable.

In looking for others with whom you want to build your village, I recommend pursuing at least one friend for virtue or confidence that is in the next life stage: Therefore, if you have young children, it's great to seek out a friend that has teenagers. If you have teenagers, it's a good idea to seek out a friend whose children are leaving the house and getting married. If your children are leaving the house and getting married, it's good to find a friend who is several years deep into grandparenting. I have learned so much from the women that are ten to fifteen years my senior; I even have a friend that I go out to lunch with who is more than two decades older than me. These friends can provide a bird's-eye view of your stage of life and help you learn from their mistakes. I remember one year when I was in one of those mismatched carpool situations that was annoying me daily, and one of my friends "in the next stage up" gave me spot-on advice that helped change my whole perspective on that matter. There is so much to learn from those who have been through our stage and survived it, and even better are the ones who thrived in it! Try not to fill your "village population" with only people your age.

Another good tip is to look for support groups that can help you get through your own personalized parenting struggles. I have several friends who rave about support groups they are in. It could be anything from a support group for parents of ADHD children, to parents of children who are having religious struggles, or even for mothers who miss their children who have gone out of town for high school.

And if there is something you are battling with in parenting that there isn't a group for—don't be afraid to go out and make a new group! If you are struggling, chances are that many others are too. At one point I came up with the idea of a support group for "wives of husbands with very demanding jobs." At the time, we had several young children ages five and under while my husband was both a junior lawyer for a large law firm and a shul *rav*. This meant he was almost never home to help me take care of our children, and this was a struggle for me. To illustrate how little we saw him during those years, on one of our wedding anniversaries my husband had to pull an office overnighter for a project, davened using a pair of backup tallis and tefillin he kept in his office, and remained there that entire next day until 10:00 PM. When he finally showed up at home, he croaked out the words, "Happy anniversary" and fell asleep pretty much on the spot.

These crazy work hours left me dealing with a whole host of unusual scenarios even beyond parenting. During one snowstorm, my husband wasn't home to shovel our cars out, and I found a ride over to a hardware store. I was in the aisle analyzing snowblowers when a friend of mine who also had a husband in the same law firm called to check on how I was handling the weather. "Well, I'm trying to figure out how to buy the right snowblower, and I have no idea how I'm going to get it home, let alone use it!" I replied. We both cracked up, and at that moment the idea for the support group was born.

The next key resident of your family's village should ideally be a *rav*, rebbetzin, *rebbi*, or former *morah* you have developed a relationship with and who knows where you are "holding" in life. These mentors can offer advice based on that knowledge of who you are and what you are capable of.

Now for a quick note on who you *don't* want to be part of your village: Anyone who makes you feel bad about yourself, makes you doubt your abilities to raise your own children, or who responds to your struggles by offering lots of criticism or a steady stream of toxic positivity should be weeded out. Which brings me to a note on "toxic positivity": There is a difference between being positive and toxically positive, just like two Advils can help you with your pain, but ten can be poisonous. We must remember, as it says in *Koheles*, there is a time and place for everything—even being sad (gasp)—and this is being said in a book on happiness! This is true of emotions as well: Putting a positive spin on everything is not always warranted, and people who blanketly do this can hurt others' feelings or even, at times, give unhelpful advice. When someone expresses distress or worry, a dismissive chipper attitude can minimize their anxiety and cause them pain.

We've all probably been on the receiving end of comments like this at some point in our lives when we felt low: someone dismissed the cause of our pain as if it wasn't a big deal when clearly it *did* feel like a big deal to us. Psychotherapist Whitney Goodman calls having an unhelpful cheerful attitude, "dismissive positivity." She recommends the following shifts when dealing with someone's mental and emotional anguish in a productive manner:

- Instead of saying, "You'll get over it," say something to impart validation and hope: "This is hard. You've done hard things before and I believe in you."
- "Think happy thoughts!" becomes, "It's probably pretty hard to be positive right now." Then you can add something like, "I'm davening for you."
- "Everything happens for a reason!" is updated to, "I know this doesn't make sense right now. Let yourself feel your painful emotions and we'll sort it all out later."

While we want to make sure to minimize hurt in our friendships and "village," it is important to point out how this warning applies to dealing with our children's pain as well. We have to understand that children are coping with different challenges than us, and different things cause them pain and distress. It's not helpful to minimize it by saying things like, "That shouldn't bother you," or "grow up." Toxic positivity can alienate people who are in pain and make them not want to open up to us in the future (which is exactly what we don't want to happen with our children). Once you identify dismissive positivity—also known as toxic positivity—it gets easier to course-correct.

Make efforts to find your village, because as much as we might like it to, it doesn't magically show up. I'll end with a humorous quote I recently saw that drives this point home: "I keep hearing it takes a village to raise a child...do they just show up or is there a number I can call immediately? I think they are having trouble finding me."

CHAPTER 33

Tool 2:
Finding Your Internal
Village—the Strength
and Love Within

*"A person should always view himself as if the
entire world depends on him."*

Zohar II 42a

*"You're always with yourself, so you might as well
enjoy the company."*

Diane Von Furstenburg

There are two opinions of the great Rabbi Akiva in two separate
Talmudic discussions that seem to contradict one another:

- In one discussion, Rabbi Akiva declares "וְאָהַבְתָּ לְרֵעֲךָ כָּמוֹךָ" to be
  "זֶה כְּלָל גָּדוֹל בַּתּוֹרָה."[1] In other words, Rabbi Akiva considers "Love
  your neighbor like [you love] yourself" to be the highest principle in the Torah.
- However, in another discussion,[2] there is debate over what to
  do if there is one water container left for two people who find

---

1   *Talmud Yerushalmi, Nedarim* 9:3.
2   *Bava Metzia* 62a.

themselves in an arid land. If they split it, neither will survive, but if one drinks it for himself then he will survive the journey back to civilization—and Rabbi Akiva rules a person should drink it himself.

Incredible! Shouldn't he have recommended splitting it with his fellow and hoping for the best (as Ben Petura rules in this same discussion) or even giving it over completely to save *the other person*? The same Rabbi Akiva who holds the elevated treatment of others in such regard so as to call it the highest principle in the Torah is saying that you should take the water for yourself and let your fellow die? How can this be?

The answer is that there is actually a "prequel" that Rabbi Akiva holds to "loving your friend like yourself." In other words, "וְאָהַבְתָּ לְרֵעֲךָ כָּמוֹךָ" is actually the *second* greatest principle of the Torah.

What then is the first? What would explain the seeming contradiction between these two disparate positions of Rabbi Akiva? The answer comes to us from the *Talmud Yerushalmi*'s next answer to the great question of what the highest principle in the Torah is. Ben Azzai brings a *pasuk* to imply that valuing *yourself* is the highest principle of the Torah.[3] After all, first man must love himself before he can love another person.

The rabbinical giants of the Mussar movement say that one of the greatest tools for growth is a process called *cheshbon hanefesh*, which is the Jewish form of soul searching. Translated literally, it means, "Making an accounting of one's soul." The process involves looking deep inside, thinking over our actions, and analyzing "how we did." We ask ourselves what we've done wrong *ben adam l'Makom* (between man and God), which involves commandments such as saying blessings and keeping kosher. We also ask ourselves what we've done wrong *ben adam l'chaveiro* (between man and his fellow), which involves prohibitions such as not gossiping and embarrassing others, and commandments such as helping our fellow man. But there is a third, oft-overlooked category, which relates to the highest principle and its prequel above.

---

3   *Talmud Yerushalmi*, *Nedarim* 9:41.

That category is called *ben adam l'atzmo* (between man and himself) and the Vilna Gaon includes this as a category of its own when dividing up the commandments. To underscore its importance, let's think for a moment about how the obligation of *cheshbon hanefesh*, introspection, fits in to all of this—it seems to belong to that third category, which reflects an obligation to oneself, resulting in improved service to God.

The obligations we have to ourselves take many different forms, and the closest Torah source we have reflecting them is from *Devarim* (4:15): "וְנִשְׁמַרְתֶּם מְאֹד לְנַפְשֹׁתֵיכֶם"—You should guard your soul greatly." Many Rabbinical commentators take this to refer to *shemiras ha'guf* (guarding one's body), but the literal meaning is referring specifically to our *nefesh* (soul). In other words, there is more to our worldly "vehicle" than our body: Our soul makes us who we really are, and we are obligated to guard it. I would like to suggest that this guarding involves first valuing and loving oneself (which involves self-care, self-confidence, and self-esteem) and appreciating the value of our own personal service to God as being imperative for the Jewish People as a whole.

Every machine needs upkeep and tweaking. Some need routine maintenance of parts, some need software updates. And therefore, it stands to reason that our personal machinery also needs spiritual updates; we need to maintain ourselves both spiritually, physically, and emotionally, and to realize how important it is to evaluate and try to fix faults, both in terms of our actions to others and toward ourselves.

It helps to be inwardly positive and loving—the same way we are to our friends and family. Rabbi Avraham Twerski says that the biggest problem facing our generation is low self-confidence/self-esteem. People think negatively and are harsh on themselves in ways they would never be to others, and yet we have to live with ourselves 24/7. Who better to develop a strong positive relationship with than your constant companion?

On the flip side, many people also don't give themselves enough positive reinforcement. How many times a week do we compliment others and offer a kind word? We should pat ourselves on the back and give caring internal feedback as well. There is a power to speaking up and verbalizing praise internally after we succeed. We can tell ourselves,

"You did a really good job in that situation," or even "Good for you for keeping your mouth shut." It's not enough to feel the feeling, the true power comes from making it meta-cognitive, or in other words, making the effort to directly bring it to mind. Don't just feel it, make yourself think it.

The reason this self-talk is of paramount importance is because our adult realities are created by our own thoughts. Another one of my favorite quotes reflects this: "Most of the battles in life are fought between your own ears." It has been shown that thoughts lead to emotions which lead to actions. So, if you are a happier person, you are likely to do better things and make healthier decisions on the whole.

But now you might ask, that's all well and good, but how do we have happier thoughts? Many Rabbinic sources tell us this comes from knowing ourselves better, and therefore, going through the process of *cheshbon hanefesh* does just that. Don't wait all the way to Rosh Hashanah to take an accounting. The *Mesilas Yesharim* recommends even doing this every day in order to "live all our days of our life in *teshuvah* (repentance)."

If doing *cheshbon hanefesh* daily sounds overwhelming, I suggest even just setting aside one car ride a week to sit in silence and review: no music, podcasts, phone calls, just your own thoughts as you drive. Think over your actions and the actions of your children and see if you are happy with what has been going on.

Rabbi Shlomo Wolbe said that a good starting point for improvement is for a person to identify their main *middah*. He taught that everyone has a special God-given character trait they are meant to excel at above all other traits. A person should identify this trait in order to use it in working on their other traits. Examples of this could be the trait of kindness, forgiveness, alacrity, or even the trait of organization.

Additionally, because of their uniqueness, the Talmud in *Sanhedrin* (37a) states that each person should tell themselves, "בִּשְׁבִילִי נִבְרָא הָעוֹלָם—The world was created for my sake." In other words, I am like a full world and I must not waste my potential. Yet, in other sources, we also have man compared to nothingness: "וְאָנֹכִי עָפָר וָאֵפֶר—I am but dust and ashes."[4] Rabbi Simcha Bunim of Peshischa explains this dichotomy by saying that a person should have two pockets, and in one they should keep the notion of "I am but dust and dirt" and in the other one, "The world was created for me." This symbolizes the importance of knowing our strengths and weaknesses; as a result, most of life's mistakes are the consequence of accidentally putting our hand in the wrong pocket for a particular situation. To prevent this, we must know ourselves!

As you do the process of *cheshbon hanefesh*, don't only make a list of your sins and shortcomings. Make a list of successes to feel proud of as well. The *Mesilas Yesharim* backs this up by saying that our *cheshbon hanefesh* should also include our good deeds. *Tzidkas Hatzaddik* says on the *pasuk* in *Shemos* (14:31), "וַיַּאֲמִינוּ בַּה' וּבְמֹשֶׁה עַבְדּוֹ"—And they believed in Hashem and in Moshe His servant," that just like you have to believe that God created the world with a purpose, so too you have to believe that you were created with a purpose as well. Taking this a step further, the *Shaarei Rachamim* quotes the *Chayei Adam* as saying that people can have a specific mitzvah to do in the world that was created just *for them* (like Shaul eradicating Amalek).[5] It is absolutely mind-boggling that a mitzvah could exist just for one person. And yet, what a strong proof of the importance of each individual person.

Here are some examples/printables:

---

4   *Bereishis* 18:27.
5   *Chayei Adam, daf* 27, from his eulogy of the Vilna Gaon.

General Cheshbon Hanefesh—One Month Log

Week	What have I done wrong?	What have I done right?	Areas I have improved on since last cheshbon?	Who have I wronged that I should apologize to?	How can I do better next time?	Roadblocks to my improvement that have come up?	How can I remove those roadblocks/set myself up for success?	Biggest success this week?
1								
2								
3								
4								

Cheshbon Hanefesh Sheet for Children

What *middos* am I succeeding with? What have I done right?	What have I done wrong?	Is there someone I need to apologize to?	What will I do next time I am in that situation again?

Lastly, look at the *cheshbon hanefesh* process as a managerial assessment for your family. This is different than figuring out how to "control yourself." Let's take the example of anger: It's probably not realistic to put it in a perfectly controlled box and say, "It will never happen again, starting now!" Instead, a managerial assessment would ask, "When it does happen again, how can I use my other personal tools and strengths to manage it?" The broader question becomes, "How are all my units working together and how can I create better synergy?"

There is a power that comes from accountability that is recognized even by leadership thinkers and executive coaches. Marshall Goldsmith, a bestselling author and leadership thinker, writes about how real change can only come from making yourself accountable for your actions, which comes from tracking them and setting aside regular intervals to check in on your progress.

There is a reason you are here, and Hashem loves you. What better reason to remember Rabbi Akiva's truly highest principle and love yourself as well?

CHAPTER 34

Tool 3:
Finding Your Fuel

"There can be no joy without food and drink."

Talmud, Pesachim 109a

"The food you eat can either be the safest and most powerful form of medicine or the slowest form of poison."

Ann Wigmore

Food is a basic building block of our physical makeup that is extremely impactful on our functioning. It is a tool for success that often becomes a "familial endeavor." Generational recipes are cherished, and holiday staples become part of the family's collective consciousness. Meals are cooked together, eaten together, and create great opportunities for family bonding. What is available in the pantry is often the foraging grounds of all family members who will therefore have similar input into their bodies. And attitudes toward food are modeled by parents.

This last point is particularly salient here. When parents are eating healthily, often children have more access to high-quality, nutritious foods and less unhealthy options to choose from when hunger hits; the saying "beggars can't be choosers" could be extended to include those who are ravenous. When my children claim to be "starving" and yet won't accept any of my healthy offerings as sustenance, I know that they are not really quite as hungry as they claim. Food is fuel and it involves family teamwork to view it as such.

The notion that food is either our medicine or our poison is important because the Western medicine world has only been catching up over the past few decades on questioning one of the biggest factors of our health: what actually goes into our bodies on a daily basis. Up until recently, American medical students had little to no education on nutrition and the powers it holds for disease prevention. Not only that, but over the last ten years or so studies have begun to show the impact of food on our mental health and happiness as well.[1] Obviously, one food choice doesn't ruin our health—our bodies have an amazing way of adapting—but over time, the more garbage we put in, the more we feel like garbage, no matter what our age may be.

It is not unusual to have a picky eater (or several) in a household. Studies show that up to thirty percent of children reject fruits and vegetables in childhood. I have a child that fits this bill: when I put a fruit in his lunchbox, I am doing little more than giving it a brief sightseeing tour away from our fruit basket. By now I must have some of the most worldly and well-traveled apples in our neighborhood.

We all know that nutrition is crucial, but what can we do about it? We really can't be there to control everything our children put in their mouths, nor do we want that burden. Additionally, it becomes challenging to make sure our children are even given healthy options once they are out of our kitchens. Over the years, I have watched with increasing alarm at the junk food many Jewish schools use to reward children for almost any reason. Thank God, there are always reasons to celebrate, and celebrating is good, but why does it have to be with our stomachs?

After the school week is done, the food fest is far from over. Shabbos arrives and many shul children's groups step in to pump children with

---

1   R.M. Warner, K. Frye, and J.S. Morrell, "Fruit and Vegetable Intake Predicts Positive Affect," *Journal of Happiness Studies*, 18 (2017): 809–826. C. Rooney, M.C. McKinley, and J.V. Woodside, "The Potential Role of Fruit and Vegetables in aspects of Psychological Well-Being: A Review of the Literature and Future Directions," *Proceedings of the Nutrition Society*, 72 (2013): 420–432.

sugar and salt while their parents daven. (I once dropped a two-year-old off at such a group, only to have a group leader shove a lollipop in his mouth without even asking him if he wanted one or whether I would allow it.) Children in such groups have only begun dusting the potato chip crumbs from their Shabbos clothes when they are sent into the *kiddush* room for a pastry and candy buffet. And this is all before they go home for lunch with Shabbos dessert, and then head off to a play-date where they may be served "Shabbos party" (another code word for sugar and carb-loading time).

The bottom line is, when we are out of our own homes, we are simply not in control of the food being offered. When it comes to healthy nutrition, it is more about arming our children with the skills to make good choices themselves, especially as they get older.

This food education boils down to the following principles: We want our children to develop intrinsic motivation for healthy eating and to self-regulate their hunger and satiety cues. We also don't want them to see food as a way to "reward" themselves or "soothe" themselves because this leads to emotional eating, which is a pattern that is hard to break later in life. We want our children to view their food choices as *neutral*, not as a value judgment. It doesn't make someone "good" or "bad" today if they are eating a certain way, despite what we often hear from adults ("I am being 'good' today, so please don't offer me a donut.").

We also want our children to be open to trying new foods, even if they don't look like what they normally eat; this skill makes life a lot easier when on vacation or at a Shabbos meal where the family cooks differently than we do. There is a photocopy of the *Talmud Yerushalmi* (*Kiddushin* 48b) on our fridge with a highlighted portion that reads, "A person will have to give an accounting of all the foods their eyes saw but did not eat." While this statement needs further exploration to understand its full meaning, for our purposes here we can learn from it that clearly our *mesorah* puts a value on trying new foods. As children get older, education includes the science behind what makes up a balanced meal or snack and what portions of carbohydrates, proteins, and vegetables are important for their particular age, size, and activity level.[2]

Let's now break this down. How many of us have told our children they have to take "four more bites" of a specific plated food before they could leave the table or have more of a different type of food? Studies actually discourage this extremely common practice because it can create a negative eating environment and prohibit children from self-regulating their hunger and satiety cues. If they say they are full and we force them to eat more, we might feel better in the moment "knowing" they *must be* full now, but we are teaching them to not trust their own bodily cues.

In addition, if we let children overfeed themselves with junk food, we are not helping them read their bodies' cues. For example, if an adult gives a child a giant-sized treat, the adult is setting up an expectation that it is OK for the child to eat the whole thing even if their body feels it's too much. After all, the child's mind says, "Well I love the taste of this, and I was given this much of it, so it must be OK to eat it all."

I have seen birthday parties where three-year-old children were handed jumbo-sized smiley-face cookies that were roughly the size of their faces (seems like this could cause even an adult a stomach ache). When I am with my four-year-old in this kind of situation, I don't take it away and make him feel different than all the other children who are chomping away. Instead, I wait for him to take several bites and then gently ask, "Is that too big for you? Do you want to continue eating it now or should we save some for later when your tummy has more room?" You might be surprised to hear that he usually says he wants to save the rest for later (by which point he will often forget about it).

We can teach children that they actually don't need to eat everything on their plate. Instead, they should just eat what they are hungry for. Two caveats to this, though. If they don't finish their dinner, I recommend putting their plate in the fridge in case they come back to you later in the evening and say they are hungry (likely looking for less healthy

---

2   Some helpful resources for teaching this can be found at: https://www.choosemyplate.gov/; https://bit.ly/3m5Jr52.

snack food). If they really are hungry, you can pull out their plate and offer them the rest of dinner, rather than give in to opportunistic snack eating. The other caveat is to only put food on their plates that we are OK with them eating in entirety; meaning if you put a hamburger and pile of fries in front of your child and they only eat the fries, it's hard to force them to back-eat the hamburger once they are already full. Better to only start with a few fries and put the rest on a separate plate. Once they are done eating what's on their plate (including the hamburger), they can have more of those separated fries if they are still hungry.[3]

The next step is to not completely restrict foods but to instead allow them in moderation. Studies have found that exercising excessive restriction can backfire later, and children who were strictly denied junk food often become overweight adults once they are able to make their own food choices.[4] However, children with no food restrictions also didn't learn balanced eating. Studies recommend applying a moderate amount of restriction to teach that all foods can be part of a balanced diet in reasonable proportions. Other studies found that labeling foods "good" or "bad" may also be bad for children's self-image when they give in to eating the "bad food."

In addition, rewarding children with food creates difficulties because it does not allow children to develop intrinsic motivation for healthy eating. However, non-food rewards can mitigate this concern. A UK study found that exposing four- to six-year-olds to vegetables and giving them a sticker for eating them was effective at increasing their vegetable intake.

When it comes to unfamiliar foods and fruit-and-vegetable consumption, parental modeling really comes into play. A survey of over 550 families found that parents' fruit and vegetable consumption was

---

3   Savage and Fisher et al., "Offering large food portions, calorically rich, sweet or salty palatable foods; the use of controlling feeding practices that pressure or restrict eating…can all undermine self-regulation of energy intake in children," *Journal of Law, Medicine and Ethics, 35(1)* (2007): 22–34.

4   M.S. Faith, K.S. Scanlon, L.L. Birch, L.A. Francis, and B. Sherry, "Parent-Child Feeding Strategies and their Relationships to Child Eating and Weight Status," *Obesity Research*, 12, 11 (2004):1711–1722.

the strongest predictor of a child's intake of those foods. Studies have also found that children are more likely to try unfamiliar foods if they observe someone they trust eating those foods (especially picked off the child's plate) while showing signs of enjoyment.

A few other tips I have found helpful in our own family:

- **Visual appeal**: Kids are more interested in fruit and vegetables when they look visually interesting and appealing. One study found that children ate more fruit when it was boat-shaped compared to fruit served simply on a white plate. Since it takes extra time, I don't do it regularly, but sometimes I indulge in creating culinary art when there is a new food I really want my children to try.

- **Dinner planning**: I have found it helpful to either let my children know ahead of time what I am planning to make that week, or to sometimes allow them to give input on Sundays for that week's dinners. Once everyone is on the same page, there is less mutiny when they arrive at the dinner table and are not in the mood for what is on their plates. After all, they were warned in advance! This also helps plan ahead so you are not scrambling with empty pots and the frantic question of "What could I possibly whip up right now?" while a mob of ravenous children return home from school. At one point, I also designated weeknights as rotations around one protein. For example, Sunday was Shabbos leftovers of usually chicken, Monday was something involving eggs, Tuesday was a recipe involving ground meat, Wednesday was a "fun" cheesy night, and Thursday was salmon night. This system further mitigates the mystery for the mutinous mobs.

- **Menu map**: Explain the proportions in a healthy meal. There are several resources that describe portion sizes and desired nutrient mix for various ages.[5] I found that after I "graduated" one of my preteens to choosing and preparing breakfast on her own, she would whine-ask, "What should I eat for breakfast?"

---

5   https://www.choosemyplate.gov/.

a lot. To solve this, I sat down with her and created a "menu" of many easy breakfast options that fit the "nutritious" bill, explaining that she could keep it on the fridge to remind her what to whip up in the morning. This proved helpful, and it can be done for other meals as well (i.e., for children who pack their own school lunches).

- **Setting up for success**: Near our backdoor, I leave a bucket filled with water bottles so my children can always grab one on their way out. This solved the problem of them becoming parched and drinking juice or soda while out (or just choosing to not drink altogether). I did the same for snacks, creating a basket of "mommy-approved munchables" that they could grab in case they got hungry while out, rather than gravitating toward vending machines or friends' lunch-box leftovers.

A note on getting "hangry": I love this term because it sums up the bad mood that many people sink into when their blood sugar lowers. Hunger can bring out intense grumpiness, especially in children who can't always sort through their bodily cues. If one of your children presents with uncharacteristic bad behavior at the same time-points every day, consider the fact that they might be hangry. I had to add a "bus snack" into one of my children's lunch boxes because of this issue. Also, for another child, I have begun to recognize the particular mood that presents when hangry, and I immediately sit them down for a snack, saying, "Just don't talk to anyone until you're done eating."

Food has come to mean many things in our society—food is love, food is security, food is fun. But it is also our fuel, and it can be a superpower that can jetpack our lives and well-being if used optimally.

CHAPTER 35

Tool 4:
Finding Your Battles—
Losing to Win

"ה׳ יִלָּחֵם לָכֶם וְאַתֶּם תַּחֲרִישׁוּן—*Hashem will do battle*
for you, you just need to keep quiet."

Shemos 14:14

"Grand strategy is the art of looking beyond the
present battle and calculating ahead. Focus on
your ultimate goal and plot to reach it."

Robert Greene

Interestingly, many aspects of parenting are commonly referred to by analogies to warfare. Just doing a quick web search I found
articles such as "The Battle to Feed Picky Children" and "Winning the
Bedtime Battle." We are not immune to these linguistic references in
our home either. When one of our children was between three and five
years old and woke us up almost every night, my husband referred to
her as a "sleep terrorist." The strange part of this phenomenon is that it
frames parents and children as "warring parties," with the connotation
of being enemies! While not very collaborative, it does reflect the level
of heavy emotion often involved. The issue with children is that they
are not fighting to be problematic or annoying; it's just hard for them

206

to see beyond what they want in the moment and to be flexible. The issue with us is that it's hard for us to take children's crying and lack of cooperation as anything other than a direct affront.

But when we take fights with our children personally, it is hard for us to step back and objectively analyze the deeper situational problem. Do we want compliance at all costs, or do we want to get to the heart of what is making our children dig their heels in and help them move through this?

And yet, there is one part of the war analogy that I do like when it comes to parenting. This is the notion of "losing battles to win wars." It is extremely helpful to try to get to the bottom of recurring arguments and fights because according to child behavioral expert Dr. Ross Greene, "Kids with behavioral challenges are lacking the skills—flexibility, frustration tolerance, problem solving—to behave in an adaptive fashion." In fact, he even has an entire method to uncovering these unsolved problems called the Assessment of Lagging Skills and Unsolved Problems (ALSUP), which can be filled out online.

Greene explains that challenging behavior occurs when the demands of the environment exceed a child's capacity to respond adaptively. This also explains why in one situation (i.e., at home) a child might be handling the demands, while in another situation (i.e., at school) they are not. The flip side could also be true. One child might do well in the school setting where everything is very structured, but not be able to handle the demands of unstructured times during weekends.

Greene lays out several plans for dealing with this, and the one I like most is effectively picking your battles. This plan involves dropping low-priority unsolved problems and putting your energy into solving the problems that precipitate challenging episodes.

As your children mature, the balancing act involves ceding more and more victories as children become more independent and need to empower themselves by following through on their own decisions. In the meantime (and while they are still young enough to need your common sense and guidance), I urge you to remind yourself the next time you feel a food/bedtime/short-term situational battle escalating: "This is not personal, and it will be over soon." Hopefully, this reminder will help you choose your battles wisely. After all, this is war...er, I mean parenting.

CHAPTER 36

Tool 5:
Finding Your Expectations

*"Train up a child in the way he should go and even
when he is old he will not depart from it."*

Mishlei 22:6

*"Our happiness depends not on what happens but
on the difference between what we expect and
what happens."*

Dr. Alex Korb

Expectations can overwhelm us when high but, much like
volume control, can provide surprising benefit when turned down. We
all know people with exceedingly high expectations, and where has that
led them? Are they the happiest people around?

With children, expectation management can be a key component in
a functioning and happy household. This applies both in terms of as-
sessing whether expectations are realistic, but also in simply explaining
what exactly they are! In other words, much of the discord often comes
from parents not clearly laying out what they expect of their child in a
given situation. Saying statements like, "I expect you to behave when
we go to the *kiddush*," is too general. It's better if you describe what
"behaving" looks like in that scenario: "I expect you to not run wildly
around the *kiddush* room, to only take one treat, and to not interrupt me

while I am talking to another adult unless it's important." This is much clearer and more effective, and you can choose whatever behaving at a *kiddush* means for your own children. The clearer you are, the more the child knows exactly what they have to do to meet the expectation (and can be held more fairly accountable if they are caught tearing through the room with a plate stacked high of cookies emblazoned with the bar mitzvah boy's personalized emblem, social security number, and sign of the zodiac, as they interrupt your conversation with the rebbetzin).

You'd be surprised how clueless children are to their parent's actual expectations. When they leave the dinner table with their plate abandoned for someone else to clear and a pool of rice beneath their seat big enough to form a California roll, you might be saying, "I can't believe I raised a slob," while they might be thinking, "What did I do that was 'slobby'?"

I have noticed that some of the major butting of heads in our household stems from behavior that significantly deviates from our expectations of how functioning human beings should act; the only problem is that it is *our* job to teach them how to *be* functioning human beings (joke's on us)! In the words of the father of one of my college friends, the "five p's" should be employed here: "Proper Planning Prevents Poor Performance." When it comes to describing proper behavior, be crystal clear—painstakingly clear—and you leave yourself a better shot at being pain-free (and maybe even with someone else polishing the crystal).

Feel free to laugh, feel free to cry, but here are some expectation charts that my husband and I created for our kids (up to age twelve) to give them a sense of what was expected during some of our critical family times and daily transition points. I will assure you that we do *not* run our family like drill sergeants! It's OK when our children don't remember everything on these lists, and they often need reminders and time to get into these routines. However, what this does quite nicely and effectively is lay out our expectations very clearly, as well as educate them about what desired behavior looks like during these situations. These lists below are just a taste. One of my other personal favorites not pictured here is "How to Respectfully Disagree with Someone."

How to Eat a Meal at Home (Regular Day)

1. Wash your hands before you eat.
2. Accept the food that is given to you, without complaint. God created seeds, someone planted them, someone harvested the crop, someone packaged it and took it all the way to your grocery store, Ima or Abba went to buy it and cooked it into a delicious meal for you. Food is fuel; enjoy this meal that will bring you energy.
3. Say a *berachah*, preferably out loud so other family members can say amen.
4. Sit in your chair, ideally facing forward, in a manner that if food falls from your mouth it will fall on your plate.
5. If you do not have a drink, straw, or certain silverware, please get what you need and see if anybody else at the table needs one of those items as well.
6. Regardless of how you enjoyed the food, make sure to thank whoever prepared it.
7. Please wait until the others eating with you have completed their first portion before requesting a second portion.
8. If you want a condiment such as ketchup or mustard, please go to the refrigerator and get it yourself.
9. Before your leave the table, say a *berachah acharonah* (blessing after eating), ideally from a *bentcher*.
10. Before your leave the table, throw out your garbage and place your dishes in the appropriate sink. Look at the floor around you to see if there is any spilled food or clutter, and if so, please clean it up, regardless of who made the mess.
11. Wash your hands if they are dirty or sticky from the food.
12. Try to stick to positive conversations and refrain from fighting, elbowing, poking, or bothering your siblings at the table. A table is like the *mizbei'ach* (altar). Let's keep it holy!

How to Eat a Shabbos Meal at Home

1. Wash your hands before you eat.
2. Accept the seat that you have been assigned without negotiation, aggression, campaigning, war-room meetings, or other general politics or warfare. Prime real estate by Ima or Abba will be rotated. Trust the process.
3. If there are guests, ask a parent how you can help (a good idea without guests as well).
4. It is good *middos* to remain at the table and participate in *Shalom Aleichem* and *Eishes Chayil* as well as *zemiros*.
5. When you wash, go back to your seat and wait until *Hamotzi*. When *Hamotzi* is made, quietly wait until the bread is given to you. Please no pushing, shoving, sprinting, or other Olympic competitions to get the first, choicest piece of challah.
6. Toys and novels are not allowed on the Shabbos table.
7. If there is something missing, like *chummus* or other dips that you would like, please feel free to get them from the fridge and offer some to others as well.
8. This is not a grape-juice-drinking, challah-eating contest. Please leave room for the other delicious and nutritious food that will be coming soon after.
9. The Shabbos table should be a positive experience and there are no bad attitudes or "table tyrant-ing" accepted. If you are upset about something, you may express it privately to a parent and they will try to help you; please refrain from wailing, hijacking the conversation to complain about others, or other public displays of annoyance. Please go to another room to calm down and return once you feel you can be part of the positive spirit of the Shabbos table.
10. If you have a *d'var Torah* or *parashah* questions, please share these before dessert/*bentching* so we make sure to have plenty of time to include these.

11. Respectfully listen to *divrei Torah*.
12. Please *bentch* out loud with a *bentcher*.
13. Before your leave the table, throw out your garbage and place dishes in the appropriate sink. Look at the floor around you to see if there is any spilled food or clutter, and if so, please clean it up, regardless of who made the mess. It is also good manners to thank whoever prepared the meal.
14. Wash your hands after you eat if they are dirty or sticky.

How to Wake Up in the Morning (Regular Days)

1. Say *Modeh Ani* and go to the bathroom to wash *negel vasser*, brush your teeth, and use the toilet. If someone else is in the bathroom, go use another available bathroom and then wait patiently to use your toothbrush from the original bathroom.
2. Get dressed before you go downstairs. Your clothes are almost always put out for you in their designated spot. Boys, make sure you have a *kippah* and tzitzis. If there is no clothing out, select something you believe would be appropriate for your day, including new socks and underwear.
3. Please throw your dirty laundry in the laundry chute rather than leave it as a carpet decoration.
4. Be mindful of other sleeping people and go downstairs without being loud in the hallway or stairway. If you are planning on staying in your room and playing before breakfast time, please be considerate by not making too much noise. In order to get to school on time you need to be in the kitchen by 7:30 AM to eat breakfast.
5. If your daily schedule requires you to daven before leaving the house, daven, from a siddur in the *cheder ha'sefarim*. If there are other people in there, don't daven loudly in a

way that could disturb them. Conflicts should be brought to a parent to resolve. Davening should be completed before breakfast.

6. For breakfast expectations, see "How to Eat a Meal at Home (Regular Day)."

7. Your shoes and coat should be at the door from the day before and your bags should be on their hooks. Locate them five minutes before we are supposed to leave and get ready by putting them on.

8. If you think you are going to need to use the bathroom during the car ride, please do so *before* we leave.

9. Remember: you are responsible for being on schedule. Set your watch alarm, check the clock, or Ima and Abba can help you with another method to set yourself up for success to be on time. Don't plan on being "nagged 'n dragged"—it's up to you to be ready on time.

10. We aim to leave the house at 8:00 AM. Please be ready by then.

How to Get Ready on Erev Shabbos

1. Make sure your Shabbos shoes are by the back door or in their designated spot.

2. Shower when you are told it's your turn. Wash your hair with shampoo and conditioner, comb through any knots and wash your entire body with soap. Please be mindful that many people are waiting for the shower and there is limited hot water on Erev Shabbos, so try not to shower for longer than fifteen minutes.

3. Ask Ima whether you should put on Shabbos clothes (this includes Shabbos socks/tights) or pajamas. Laundry goes to the laundry chute and your towel goes to its hook after

you are done drying off. Please do not leave it marinating on the carpet for Shabbos.

4. Put your *d'var Torah* by your seat, and your *parashah* questions by Abba's seat.

5. Clean your room. Make your bed, remove all debris from the floor, and place any remaining dirty laundry in the chute.

6. Clean up the playroom and turn off the *muktzah* toys. It does not matter whose mess it is.

7. Gather personal items that have been left around the house (including books, toys, school papers you want to keep, etc.) and put them back in your own room.

8. Ask Ima and Abba if they need help with anything.

9. Please let Ima know on Friday morning if there is a specific playmate you want to invite over. Please do not wait until the last minute and then be upset if you don't have plans on Shabbos.

10. Please be mindful that Erev Shabbos is a very busy time and a lot needs to get done. This is like the "extra bonus round" of a game show—your help and cooperation is extra appreciated on Erev Shabbos!

Creating Your Own "How-To" Chart

* Pick something that your family has been struggling with.
* Try to break it down into as many easy and manageable pieces as possible, but not too many that it becomes overwhelming.
* Try to think of points of tension that have been coming up in the situation and figure out solutions that you put in the list. For example, we found there was drama when a child ended up without a playdate but hadn't expressed any interest in one before Shabbos. That is why we included, "Please let Ima know on Friday morning if there is a specific playmate you want to invite over."

- Post the chart somewhere that the whole family will see it before a given scenario comes into play (for example, put it in the center of the dinner table before dinner or put it on the fridge on Friday before Shabbos).
- Laminate the ones that you will need frequently and consider handing them out each week at the time they are needed (for example, Erev Shabbos tasks).

CHAPTER 37

Tool 6:
Finding Your Voice

"‎וְאַחַר הָרַעַשׁ אֵשׁ לֹא בָאֵשׁ ה׳ וְאַחַר הָאֵשׁ קוֹל דְּמָמָה דַקָּה"—

*After the earthquake a fire; but Hashem was not
in the fire. And after the fire, a small, still voice."*

Melachim I 19:12

*"There is a voice inside of you that whispers all day
long, 'I feel that this is right for me, I know that
this is wrong.'"*

Shel Silverstein

My friend Debbie is a high school librarian by day and health coach
by night. This means she spends her time empowering herself with new
information, but with the backdrop of a whole lot of whining from the
people around her.

Debbie is incredibly insightful, so when she introduced me to the concept of voices from childhood that get trapped in our heads, I was really
taken by it. After all, it explained a lot. How else could I function like a
mature, adult individual in most of my life but when I was confronted
by a flash sale on new Shabbos clothes be taken over by the primal,
unrefined instinct of, "I have to buy some!"

"It's the toddler in you throwing a tantrum," Debbie explained. "It
wants what it feels like having *now*, and it can't see past the present

216

moment to take into account the bigger picture of what you want the *most* (which is to be financially responsible and save up for more important things)."

The concept of the general voice in our head, the one that narrates and judges our lives, is not new. In fact, it has gotten a lot of press lately, especially in the field of meditation and relaxation to quiet that constant chatter of our inner consciousness. Dan Harris, Author of *10% Happier*, writes about the moment when he was lying in bed and realized the mean-spirited nature of "the voice in my head—the running commentary that had dominated my field of consciousness since I could remember." Harris talks about how after that, he felt he needed to find a way to separate from that unkind voice in order to get more control over his inner critic.

We all have internal narration, but we can break it up further to understand that the voice that chooses to speak up inside us is not always consistent—sometimes it's our inner toddler speaking up and sometimes it's our inner teenager. The Internal Family Systems (IFS) approach developed by Harvard psychologist Richard Schwartz, which we referenced in section 1, views each person as containing a network of subpersonalities struggling with each other. These internal subpersonalities include voices like the "inner critic," the "taskmaster," the "perfectionist," and the "underminer," which speak up and even fight with each other in different situations. The reason it is helpful to learn and understand these categorizations is that it helps us figure out how to respond to these inner promptings, especially when they are not serving us well.

For example, to deal with our "inner toddler" voice we need to speak to it like we would to a toddler. "I know you want the new Shabbos clothes, but you really don't need them, I'm sorry." And then we need to be firm and consistent with it, even while it is mid-tantrum. "I am the adult here. I know what's best for you." You might find distraction also helps with this voice as it screams inside you, just like it is often helpful with a toddler. However, instead of dangling a bright toy in front of your eyes and saying, "Oooooo, bet you can't grab this!" you might just leave the website with the flash sale and say, "OK, it's time to put the laundry away." Once you are out of the room, your temptation is likely to stop calling you.

The same is true of our internal teenage voice. When it's rebelling against our inner common sense, we need to enforce rules with it like we would for a teenager. For example, let's say the house is finally quiet and your exhausted self knows you really should go to bed, but you are also enjoying the silence and tempted to finally have some "me time." The inner voice whispers, "I'll just sit down for a few minutes and read, or organize this room, or call my friend in another time zone, or all the other things I like to do when I finally have some time at night...And then I'll go to sleep." Most of the time when we sweet-talk ourselves into this kind of unwise behavior, we know we are going to end up staying awake for two hours; in reality, we are happily deluding ourselves from the start. Your responsible inner voice contradicts, "Just go to sleep, this really is the time you need to get to bed," and your teenage voice pipes up and screams, "I'm not going to listen to you. I want to have some time to myself while the house is quiet!" and the next thing you know it's midnight and as you hit the pillow and dread your alarm, which is set for 6:00 AM, your last thought is, "I can't believe I did that again."

And so, if you are able to recognize the teenage voice popping up inside you, lay down the law. "No, this is your pillow curfew. You need to get to bed now so you will function tomorrow. We can't just do whatever we feel like, we need to remember that our actions have consequences."

It's helpful to realize that even as adults and parents, we never leave our childhood totally behind—the voices from our younger years still echo within us and affect our decisions. This helps us to have extra patience with our children, because we, too, have those internal tendencies to act out, want something now with reckless disregard for the future, and even just illogically stay up way past our bedtimes.

My husband once rolled his eyes at me as I made a bad decision in an area that I was struggling with for quite some time. I quickly reminded him of the *Talmud Yerushlami* on the *pasuk* in *Mishlei* (3:26) "כִּי ה׳ יִהְיֶה בְכִסְלֶךָ," where it explains this to mean that God will be with you even when you are doing silly, unwise things: "Hashem is with me when I make a bad decision, so why can't you be?" I asked. "Don't forget we're supposed to emulate Hashem!"

He smiled, but he got the message loud and clear. It's not easy to always make the right decisions, and sometimes the toddler and teenager voices inside of us simply just win over our adult common sense.

There are also other approaches to dealing with these internal voices, especially the inner critic after we know we've made an unwise decision. Ethan Kross, of the University of Michigan's Emotion and Self-Control Lab, explains that one of the best ways to deal with these different voices inside is to use a popular CBT approach called "self-distancing." This involves answering the voices that are not serving us well from a detached perspective—almost as if there is another person inside of us responding to them. For example, let's say after staying up late again, you are exhausted the next day and feel bad about having let your internal "teenage voice" convince you yet again to do something unwise. Instead of beating yourself up, you can speak internally, replacing "I" with "you," and say something like, "Beth, it's no surprise you gave in to the desire to stay up late yet again to have some quiet personal time. It makes sense. Now that you realize it's happening too often and impacting your day by being tired, I know you'll find a way to work personal time into the day as opposed to relying on it late at night."

Another approach to dealing with the inner critic voice is to use "story editing."[1] As I wrote in probably my most famous article, "Life is comprised of the stories we tell ourselves."[2] In other words, we are constantly telling ourselves tales about what is going on around us that impacts our realities. Brené Brown's research shows that whenever we feel threatened by anxiety, fear, shame, or even loss, our brains immediately and automatically demand a story to make sense out of the difficult situation. According to Brown, the problem is that these stories usually exaggerate our greatest fears, shame triggers, and insecurities.

---

1   T. D. Wilson, *Redirect: The Surprising New Science of Psychological Change* (Little Brown/ Hachette Book Group, 2011).

2   Beth Perkel, "The Pain of Parting," *Mishpacha* magazine, January 1, 2020.

Those "trigger stories" are just our first drafts though, which Brown uses strong language to describe as poor versions of the actual reality.

MINDSET MALFUNCTION

The first story we tell ourselves about a situation is usually the worst, both when we are interpreting ours and other people's actions and motives. However, when we realize this was just our rough first draft and we are allowed a rewrite, we can get in the habit of editing and then retelling the story to ourselves in a kinder light. For example, when we look forward to a wonderful evening with our children and then find the fabric of familial society quickly unweaving as sibling fights and complaining begin, instead of telling ourselves, "I'm a failure. I have no control over my kids. I will never be able to get through this evening without yelling at them." We can rewrite the story to explain what really happened. For example, "Taking care of children is not easy. It's OK to be frustrated, especially when my perfect vision for the evening didn't play out. But I am motivated and can keep working at it, which makes me far from a failure."

Once we recognize the voices that make up our internal world, we can also be kinder to our internal critic, knowing that we all have our "moments" and need understanding. Parenting is difficult, and sometimes the same tools are needed to work on raising ourselves, even as adults. Finding your voice means choosing the one inside of you that gets to speak up over all the other internal chaos; that "voice of reason" that acts as the still, thin sound in our lives, overpowering our baser nature and childhood instincts that still try to tantrum toward getting their way. Tame your critic, learn how to respond to your inner child and other voices that pop up, and you will find that you are actually able to rewrite the story of your internal life.

CHAPTER 38

Tool 7:
Finding Your Flow

*"The Jewish idea of 'relaxing' means to tune into
another aspect of living. It should be purposeful
and directed."*

Aish.com

*"Realize that now, in this moment of time, you are
creating. You are creating your next moment."*

Sara Paddison

Time at home with everyone puttering around the house can sometimes seem endless. Not to mention when there is the background mel-
ody of whiny voices calling out "I'm bored" as the soundtrack. Finding
your flow as a household is about figuring out how to get everyone into
regular patterns of using their "downtime" in the best ways, ideally
turning it into a tool. As we noted earlier in this book, boredom is not a
bad thing for children. It's often when their creative juices get flowing
and they think on a deeper level. In other words, when the "world is
off" around them (meaning they aren't running around, and/or visual
stimuli such as technology isn't stealing their attention), they turn to
internal stimuli such as thoughts and ideas.

I came across this excellent use of an acronym for "bored" that I really
think captures great ideas for family home time. Feel free to use this

one or create your own. I put a picture of this acronym on our centrally located project-board. You can print out a few and put them in whatever areas catch your children's attention (fridge, stairway landing, back door):

> **B** een creative?
> **O** utside play?
> **R** ead a book?
> **E** xercised twenty minutes?
> **D** one something helpful?

Here's one I created myself:

> **L** earned some Torah?
> **A** ctive time?
> **Z** oned out, and had some creative thoughts?
> **Y** awned, realized you woke up too early, and went back to sleep?

Some other ideas I like to implement during family free-flow time are:

- Keep a bin of random recyclables that, with a little creativity, can be morphed into great projects and activities. I found cardboard packaging inserts that we were able to make into jewelry boxes, bubble wrap that became a popping road to run across and scooter over, and an empty tube structure inside a Costco foil-roll that became a royal scepter (complete with its own plastic stand) before Purim. This creativity does not at all have to come from you. The best thing is to let your children loose in the bin when they are bored and allow them to create from those recyclables on their own.
- Unless something is intricate and worth saving, I personally find the shelf life of school projects to be about one week. The only problem is that my children get a bit offended when they find their school masterpieces in the trash. After a lot of back and

forth, I found a solution that ekes out a little longer and doesn't clutter up your dining room table-turned-museum display case. We bought a high-quality empty frame from the "reject pile" of a custom framing store (in our case it was Michaels) and with some wire, screws, and decorative clothes pins (also available at Michaels), we turned it into an art display frame. To do this, place screws in the back on each side of the frame, wind the wire from around one screw across the back to the other, hang it on the wall, and voilà! You now have a line to pin the art with a beautiful custom-quality frame surrounding it. Ours has two rows but depending on how big the frame is, you can do more. We rotate the projects periodically (or give the curation of the display as a fun task to the next child in the house who calls out "I'm bored").

- Indoor treasure hunt: No need to spend time hiding things yourself; just use existing items in the house. Examples include:
  - "Find as many things as you can in the next fifteen minutes that are purple."
  - "Find as many toy cars as you can" (great for cleaning up/reorganizing—after they find them, put them all in a designated "car" bin).
  - "Find as many library books as you can" (helpful gathering bonus for you too!).
  - "Find toys you used to love and haven't played with in a long time and give them to a younger sibling."

  Give the child who finds the most a small prize.
- Put on a play: Children can create simple plays or more elaborate ones. If you are feeling adventurous, use clothes from your closet as costumes. The only caveat is you have to be willing to sit through the show...
- Learn a new way to do art with a "how-to": There are plenty of how-to art videos online or challenges like the "Three-Marker Challenge" that kids get really into. There are also many books that can teach skills like step-by-step drawing or paper folding.

Have older children help with a project like origami to minimize frustration for the younger children.

- Create tower challenges, such as toothpick towers with mini marshmallows and toothpicks, stacks of index cards that can be folded in any way to make it tallest, or deck-of-cards towers.

- Pen pals: Write a letter to a grandparent or match up pen pals between one of your children and the child of a friend that lives out of town. Even in today's fast-paced world of communication, there is a sense of magic in receiving a handwritten letter in the mail. If your child doesn't have much to say in his or her letter, suggest writing part of a made-up story and then mail it to the pen pal to write the next part, and so on. At the end, they will have a joint creation.

Conclusion:
Light at the End
of the Tunnel

There is a *Rabbeinu Bechaye ben Asher* in *Parashas Ki Seitzei*[1] that brings a *midrash* detailing how each soul, before it comes into the world, is shown its entire future journey on earth. This preview of the future includes all the things that will happen to it (including who its family will be), and the soul both agrees with and desires these things in order to come down to earth. I am struck by the beauty of this idea because it reminds us that no matter how hard children are to raise, no matter how foreign they seem to us in any given stage, or no matter what struggle we are helping them through that we never dreamed of dealing with, our particular children were meant for us. After all, their specific souls desired to be with us during their time in this world.

There is a myth out there that everyone else has "got it together," has jumped on the happiness train, and is riding out into a breathtaking sunset in between the delightful toots of the engine's whistle. The problem with this fallacious image is that this mythical train has no real destination. The destination is within you: only you have the power to make yourself happy and well adjusted, and it doesn't just happen by itself. It takes skills. It takes slowing down. It takes noticing, tasting, feeling, reveling in the joy of the small moments we previously missed, the step-by-step changes that alter our lifetimes and provide us lifelines.

---

1   *Devarim* 22:8.

We have now studied countless components together that, once implemented, can provide so many tools for you and your children to attain happiness: grit, timeline perspective, emotional agility, perspective, mindfulness, habit installation, patience, gratitude, acceptance, and identifying individual strengths. We discussed new language for our homes: choosing the key terms our families stand for, reducing complaining, reframing situations, and talking through other people's perspectives. We discussed becoming comfortable with some previously uncomfortable things: being vulnerable and letting our children fail when warranted. We discussed setting ourselves up for success in our surroundings: more time outside in nature and choosing visuals in our homes that spark joy. We studied setting ourselves up for success with our time: losing the rush, better routines, explaining expectations, and more mindful unstructured time at home. We explored setting ourselves up for success with our social/emotional needs as parents: making time for friendships, finding our "village," and true self-care. We learned to dig deeper to understand our children as individuals with their particular personality types, strengths, Pilot Light Motivations, mindset malfunctions, outlook frames, and predispositions. We now have exercises that are small enough to incorporate every day for our own "joy breaks," and have a clear goal to aggregate all the gains we can get by every new habit and tool we are able to successfully install in our home lives. God willing, all of this will maximize our families' happiness.

We covered many lessons together, and we now have a plan of action. Start with working on one chapter for two weeks, and then build as you go, adding the key topic in the next chapter every two weeks thereafter. In this way, you will have planted all the seeds within one year! After this, the idea is to keep expanding and building on each topic in whatever manner works best for your family. Remember the lesson of the British cycling team: even marginal gains, when added together, can transform you into champions. So never underestimate the power of small changes.

You can do this. The fact that you took the time to read this book to the very end means you are both growth-minded and motivated, which

I would say is half the recipe for success right there. Life is driven by momentum, and taking that first step is always the hardest. After that, you have already pushed yourself into motion and can rely on Newton's first law: A body in motion will stay in motion. Keep going, don't stop!

Once we have done all we can to prepare our children for the life that awaits them, we need to foster independence and help them make the transition to their own journey through the *prozdor*. I once heard someone analogize parenting to filmmaking: First we are our young children's directors, telling them exactly what to do, where to stand, and how to act. Then as they become teenagers, we shift to the role of their producers, giving them guidance from behind the scenes but letting the actual scenes play out as they bring their own talents, actions, mistakes, and skills to the forefront. And finally, as they reach adulthood, we become merely consultants, here to guide when it is asked of us.

There is a mindfulness exercise in which a person is told to close their eyes, picture something worrying them and mentally place it in a balloon. After they have done this, they are asked to let the balloon go and watch it float up into the sky, out of their reach.

Let's try and remember this image when it comes time to give our children more space and to trust them to use the skills we have given them as they go off on their own. They are our greatest creations—but ultimately, when we let go of the balloon and let it float out into the distance, we are putting them in the hands of God just like we have done every day before, even when they were young and we *thought* we were in control. As such, no matter what wind may toss them about, and no matter what tailspin may put them out of your grasp, we know they will land exactly where they are supposed to journey: through the tunnel of life, where the light you have wired them for in childhood will now ultimately illuminate the winding path ahead leading toward the banquet hall.

שֵׁם עוֹלָם אֶתֶּן לוֹ אֲשֶׁר לֹא יִכָּרֵת

In a year of darkness, we seek light, and remember those that are no longer among us.

For the many precious members of B'nei Yisrael and the world at large who were lost in the coronavirus pandemic, may this book serve as a memorial.

And also, for my four *neshamos tehoros* that reached the end of the tunnel before its beginning.

Among those are my identical twins that didn't make it past the second trimester this year. Legacies come in many forms, and this book was completed at the hour of midnight on a day you may have very well otherwise been born.

For all four, even though I never had the joy of holding you in my arms, I still am and forever remain your mother. This book, also a labor of love, is dedicated in your memory.

My sincere hope is that you are enjoying another light, the Divine Light, that someday will welcome us all at the end of the Tunnel.

Beth Perkel

About the Author

Known for her bright smile and ever-present laugh, Beth Perkel is a noticeably happy person. She is also a professional writer, mediator, and teacher, and was a shul rebbetzin for almost a decade. She was first published in national and international magazines by age seventeen, won her first writing award at age eighteen, and had her writing included in a New York Times bestselling book by age nineteen. Perkel's education in and passion for psychology began during her years at the University of Pennsylvania, where she graduated Phi Beta Kappa and conducted funded national and international psychology research. Since then, she has written in-depth articles, stories, and first-person essays for a dozen online and print publications. Her work has been featured in *Newsweek Magazine*, *Chicago Tribune*, *Mishpacha Magazine*, *Family First*, *Aish.com*, *Times of Israel*, *The Jewish Press*, and in many books. Perkel also loves giving *shiurim*, cooking Moroccan food, and winning snowball fights. She lives in Chicago with her husband and children.